AN INTERNATIONAL PEACE COURT

AN INTERNATIONAL PEACE COURT

DESIGN FOR A MOVE FROM STATE CRIME TOWARD WORLD LAW

by

THOMAS HOLTON

INTRODUCTION
by
GEORGE W. KEETON

MARTINUS NIJHOFF / THE HAGUE / 1970

ISBN 978-94-011-8181-5 ISBN 978-94-011-8826-5 (eBook)
DOI 10.1007/978-94-011-8826-5

For My Aunt

Roseline Foley

ACKNOWLEDGMENTS

This book is a development and expansion of selected aspects of the author's dissertation at the Yale Law School, in the course of writing which he was fortunate to be able to benefit from the interest and counsel of Professors Harold Lasswell, Leon Lipson, Egon Schwelb and, in particular, Myres McDougal. Professor McDougal's professional and personal commitment to the values of human dignity, as well as to the relevance of law as an instrument of their enhancement, has been a singular source of inspiration.

The late Professor Lyttleton Fox of the Seton Hall University School of Law was a most cherished friend and encouraging presence. He read the manuscript and offered valued criticism and suggestions. Albert Garretson, Professor of Law and Director of the Institute of International Law at New York University School of Law, also very kindly read the manuscript and offered important advice and encouragement.

A special debt of gratitude is owing to Professor George W. Keeton of London University for the thought and empathy that went into his writing of the Introduction.

Cordial thanks go to Mr. Frederick Martin, an old friend and to Professor Philip Bouchard of Marquette University School of Law for their technical advice, to Helen Adamson, Vadie James and Maureen Johnson for their secretarial service, and to Messrs. James Hand, Larry Abrahamson and Stephen Barr, students of the University of Wyoming College of Law, for their proof-reading assistance.

Finally, the author wishes to acknowledge the long-suffering of his wife, Leah, and his children, John, Karen, Glyn, Susan and Bryce, in the face of the competing demands upon his time made by this book.

. . . the search must be in terms of specific formulae, not merely in resolutions that proclaim the brotherhood of man.

Justice William O. Douglas

TABLE OF CONTENTS

INTRODUCTION

The classical concept of International Law, as developed by Gentilis, Grotius and their successors, accepted as its starting point the sovereignty of states, from which it followed that (1) the rules of International Law were based upon the general consent of those states; and (2) that, since state sovereignty was not capable of limitation, otherwise than by the consent of the state itself, in the last resort, International Law must accept the fact of war. Two world wars within the space of thirty years, and the development of nuclear weapons of unlimited potential, have compelled statesmen and lawyers to take a fresh look at the foundations of international relations. The First World War was followed by the creation of the League of Nations, and by the establishment of the Permanent Court of International Justice. The failure of both, insofar as the preservation of peace was concerned, was apparent in the continuance of international insecurity, culminating in World War II. This again was followed by the establishment of a new international organisation, the United Nations, with its auxiliary, the International Court of Justice. Nevertheless, international security seems further away than ever, and it may be suggested that it is the devastating potential of nuclear weapons, rather than the strength of international machinery, which has so far prevented a third general conflict far more disastrous than either of the two World Wars which have already taken place.

In this book, Professor Holton rightly ascribes the continuing international insecurity primarily to the attachment of the major powers to their distinctive, and at times, conflicting policies. Any international organisation which is based upon these differences contains in itself an inherent contradiction which cannot be resolved. Further, all lesser states develop a progressive feeling of frustration, on account of their inability to change, or even to modify appreciably, these basic attitudes of the super-powers. Coincidentally, the actions of the super-powers themselves in the Security Council of the United Nations often fail to produce any positive result towards the preservation of peace, for lack of the unanimity necessary before a Security Council resolution on a question of substance can become operative. One important difference between the United Nations and its predecessor, the League of Nations, is that in the United Nations the power-gap between the great powers and the rest is so very much larger.

In the sphere of international law, there is also a difference between the activities of the Court of International Justice and its predecessor, the Permanent Court of International Justice. References to the present court are fewer, and of less international consequence, than references to the earlier court, possibly because of the belief of potential litigants that in any but the most trifling disputes, the machinery for the enforcement of a judgment is likely to be wanting, again for lack of unanimity among members of the Security Council. In any event, the jurisdiction of the Court of International Justice, like that of its predecessor, is an extremely limited one. From both, there have been excluded those disputes which are likely to lead to war, inasmuch as they are deemed to affect the vital interests of states.

It is the particular merit of Professor Holton's book that he offers a way out by a proposal which, at one and the same time, meets the old criticism that the enforcement of a compulsory international jurisdiction would lead to wars, rather than to their avoidance; which also meets, to a considerable extent, the criticism, that international affairs, especially in the area of potential conflicts, are the province of the statesman, and not of the lawyer or judge; and which, finally, will do something to modify the feeling of frustration which nationals of small states feel, in watching from the side-lines, the conflicting policies of major powers.

Professor Holton boldly advocates the establishment as soon as possible of an International Peace Court with *compulsory* jurisdiction in respect of any major act of violence by any state. If a state should fail to appear when summoned there could be judgment by default. The judgments of such a court (for which Professor Holton has prepared a model statute) would not have, and would not be intended to have, any sanctioning machinery to support them. They would remain moral judgments only, although achieved by legal means. At the same time, Professor Holton believes that they would focus world opinion, and especially the opinion of smaller powers, upon the wrongdoer more decisively than any existing international machinery, and that they would win greater acceptance.

At first sight, the absence of any mechanism of enforcement, although avoiding the criticism that attempts to enforce such judgments might provoke conflicts, would appear to be a major weakness, but against this should be weighed the following points, which reinforce the moral authority of the proposed court:

(a) absence of the threat of enforcement will permit judgments to be made upon the fact of a case without fear of violent consequences;

(b) the necessity for a state which has been guilty of violence either to justify its act in terms of law, or suffer judgment by default, will in itself act as a restraint; and if a case is argued, the facts can be established in a judicial manner; and not as at present, in the Security Council and the Assembly, by reference to political considerations;

(c) judges will sit, not as national delegates, but as lawyers of distinction, free from national attachments. In both the Assembly and the Security Council, the members are active agents of the states which they represent. They explain, and they are expected to explain, the attitude of the state from which they derive their authority.

One point which is worthy of consideration is that the publication of a regular series of reports of a tribunal such as Professor Holton describes would have a considerable impact, over a substantial period of time, as a record of violent infractions of International Law.

There are some interesting problems arising out of Professor Holton's proposal which merit consideration. One of them is that of provocation; another is the question whether an attack upon one state from the territory of another is an attack by the neighbouring state, or is an unauthorised expedition. In the latter case, there may arise a further question whether the state from which it proceeds has been guilty of negligence in failing to prevent it. In these cases, which have in the past been so often productive of international friction, the establishment of the facts by an independent judicial tribunal has a value which is self-evident.

Professor Holton's scholarly and thoughtful contribution merits close attention as a positive suggestion, designed to isolate the wrongdoer, and to focus public opinion, without setting in motion machinery which might in the long run be productive of further international conflicts.

GEORGE W. KEETON

17th October 1969

I

THE RELEVANCE OF LAW

Responsibility for a Law of Peace

Knowledge creates responsibility. The present work proceeds from the conviction that our knowledge of law, meaning the whole legal process, painfully developed through centuries of trial and error and review, should be applied to the solution of the most serious problem confronting modern man – international violence.

This is no truism. Almost all of us probably would relegate responsibility for international peace to politics and diplomacy rather than to law. Armed fights between nations seem to be not inherently a legal concern.[1] Law rather seems to belong with lesser matters.

The conviction behind the present offering is that a breach of the peace is just as much a legal problem between nations as it is between individual persons. More so, in fact, because nations can do more harm to public order than can individuals. Conversely, nations may in some respect be more amenable to legal control than individuals.

To say that international violence is a legal problem is somewhat like saying that a disease is a medical problem. The latter assertion is true whether or not a medical procedure currently exists for curing the disease. Disease is a medical problem because it attacks the health of the physical body which medical science and art profess to protect. Violence, correspondingly, is a legal problem because it attacks the health of the body politic which the science and art of law profess to protect. If no effective legal procedure exists to control the problem of international violence, it becomes our responsibility to invent one,

[1] See McDougal and Feliciano, *Law and Minimum World Public Order* 2–3 (1961), noting the common attitude which "affirms that man's destructive impulses and instruments of violence have escaped all bounds and that little or nothing can be done by law....," and seeing this attitude as,

> a particular piece of the contemporary disillusionment which characteristically minimizes the actual and potential function of law in the world power process, exaggerates the role of naked power, and deprecates continuing concern with legal principles and procedures of legalism....

just as we have done, with substantial, though obviously not complete effectiveness, for the problem of domestic violence.

It is not enough, however, to pay lip service to this responsibility. The practical concern is with its placement and format.

The Placement of Responsibility

The ultimate responsibility for developing the legal control of transnational violations of the peace will devolve upon all of us. The immediate responsibility rests upon those who by reason of tradition, experience and role in society are best equipped to offer leadership.

The leadership required for the effective exercise of this responsibility can be expected to come particularly from lawyers and legal scholars. The most fateful challenge, said Professors McDougal and Feliciano, addressing their fellow lawyers, is that of

> inventing the structures of authority and sanctioning procedures designed most economically to move the peoples of the world from our immediate, precarious balance of terror toward minimum security and a more complete world public order of human dignity, and after investigating controlling conditions, of recommending the measures in communication and other action most effectively calculated to affect the predispositions of leaders and peoples to accept these structures and procedures and to put them into practice.[2]

One cannot call upon the legal profession for leadership, however, without being aware that any long-term legal response commensurate with the problem of international violence will call for a broad base of concern and support, one importing a widely diffused understanding among all people of the function of law in the society.

This requirement of understanding cannot be noted without candidly recognizing the need for improvement in existing methods for the production and distribution of knowledge of the legal process. The need is for both better research into the operation of the law and better education in law, professional as well as general. On the assumption that law is as essential to the viability of the world society as are science and technology, the need for research and education in law might realistically be assimilated to the now widely appreciated need which our society has for both scientific research and scientific education, professional as well as general. Indeed, unless our legal understanding can soon catch up with our technological understanding, we may not have long to enjoy the blessings of the latter.

The actual situation as to legal research and education, exposed by

[2] *Id.* at 260.

a law school dean, Bayless Manning, in an address in March, 1968, is that American law schools are virtually without research funding, as major "sources that support research into virtually every other area of human activity by and large have been predominantly inhospitable to legal research."[3] To which Dean Manning reacted with this incisive query:

> Is it a plausible proposition that the operation of our legal institutions is somehow different and not worth serious research investigation? According to the latest annual report of the university with which I am associated, total university expenditures for research last year amounted to more than 37 million dollars; of that amount more than 10 million dollars was devoted to medical research – and less than 20 thousand dollars was attributed to legal research. These research ratios are nationally typical. Is the health of our legal order today so robust that we can afford such unconcern about it?
>
> ...we know remarkably little about how the legal process actually operates and we also know that with an investment of time and money, we could find out a great deal about it.[4]

Legal knowledge need not be kept esoteric.[5] If modern man's adjustment to his environment demands a basic understanding of science, does it not equally demand a basic understanding of the legal process?[6] In the present work an appeal for such understanding in support of the responsibility for a new enterprise in designing and operating an adequate international legal process is implicit.

The Format of Responsibility

The abstract solution can be tempting for its vagueness and the concrete solution can be reproached for its unfamiliarity. The format of the new responsibility, however, should be shaped neither by the temptation nor by the reproach.

The Temptation Of The Abstract

The tempting feature of an abstract proposal is that it is not too

[3] Manning, "New Tasks For Lawyers," address before a Conference on Law and the Changing Society, sponsored by the American Bar Association and the American Assembly of Columbia University, Chicago, Illinois, March 14, 1968.

[4] *Ibid.*

[5] See Barkun, *Law Without Sanctions* 1 (1968):

> Indeed, law has always appeared as one of society's mysteries, hedged about with taboos and frequently cloaked from public view, but the development of mysteries is part and parcel of the process of professionalization.

[6] See American Assembly, *Report on Law and the Changing Society* 9 (1968):

> Instruction in law and legal processes should be a part of primary, secondary and college education. The legal profession should encourage programs of such instruction.

difficult to get the various nations to accept it. It costs little to pass a resolution proclaiming the brotherhood of man. The price of a concrete proposal, on the other hand, is that it may displace something else, something familiar and invested in.

The responsibility for designing a legal process for controlling international violence cannot be discharged in the formulation of an abstract system of total order which by reason of its abstractness would speak over the head of modern man and fail to address him in his existential predicament. The philosopher, Gabriel Marcel, captured this insight:

> And when I was still very young I grasped the truth that it is impossible to build true peace on abstractions... the fact that it is impossible to build true peace on abstractions is the deepest reason for the failure of the League of Nations...[7]

One truth that we can retrieve from our experience with the League of Nations is that the goal of international peace and security cannot be encompassed in one great leap forward. Such a leap could only be a move in the abstract, severed from the real world of partial consensus which exists among nations. The alternative approach is one of modest but concrete steps. If beset modern man is to be talked into making the first step, he must be met where he is to be found in his existing environment. This means, in particular, that any design of action seeking to be realistic, must respect the present locale of limited international consensus which is available to support any concrete undertaking for peace and security.

The Reproach Of The Unfamiliar

At the same time the new design need not be dictated by the inertia of the familiar order in its resistance to innovation.[8] One expects the reproach of unfamiliarity to be raised against any new proposal for a more serviceable world legal process. But the traditionalist objection may be countered with the words of Professor Arthur Sutherland:

> The familiar is not the necessary. What has been habitual in the law and in education for it may be deadening if it fails to accord with new demands of society.[9]

[7] Marcel, *Man against Mass Society* 3–4 (Fraser Translation, Gateway, 1962).

[8] See Boulding, *The Impact of the Social Sciences* 111 (1966):
Social systems, like all other systems, have momentum. They tend to continue, that is, long after the initial force which gave rise to them has disappeared.

[9] Sutherland, *The Law At Harvard* 369 (1967).

The Present Design

The present design attempts a concrete answer to the nearly universal desire for some practical step toward a peaceful and secure community of nations. It is disciplined by an awareness of the environment of negative perspectives and practices which condition the possibility for broad-based agreement by nations to work together to build world order. At the same time it seeks to husband certain positive lines of force found in present perspectives and practices, lines converging in the trend toward greater allocation of responsibility for international order to entities organized on a less than universal base of consensus. For entities such as regional agencies and multinational conventions have shown that the consensus of a limited number of nations can benefit still other nations. The European Common Market has benefited nations in Africa. The Nuclear Test Ban Treaty has benefited nations whose governments have not subscribed to it.

Our world neighborhood needs the creativity which will bring together the available forces of international consensus in support of a procedure for deterring the unauthorized resort to international violence. To be effective such a procedure must make violence less rewarding to its perpetrators, that they may perceive less to be gained by resort to violence than by respect for law.

Our search, therefore, is not simply to create a model for a respectable world order,[10] but to design an approach to it. The question we have to answer is how do we get from here to there. The answer presented in these pages is: by way of an International Peace Court.

The reason for proposing the use of an impartial tribunal as the step toward a better legal order, is that the structural demands of a tribunal, compared with those of other instrumentalities, are modest in relation to their effective potential. A court would not demand so much input of international consensus or resources as to prove unrealistic. At the same time it may be able to deliver a sufficient output of deterrence as to be effective.

Not too much input of consensus would be demanded, in that the enterprise could be launched without having to get the agreement of all the nations, even of all the major ones. That this can be envisaged within the existing structure of authority, as given historically in the

[10] See, e.g., Clark and Sohn, *World Peace Through World Law* (3d ed. 1966). See also Starke, *An Introduction To The Science Of Peace (Irenology)* 194–203 (1968) for a list of such models.

United Nations Charter and construed through time to favor the living need over the dead letter, is part of the argument offered for consideration herein. Moreover, the only consensus required of participating nations is the agreement to maintain a court, not a military establishment, nor a program of economic sanctions nor even a course of diplomatic pressure. The only resources demanded are those required to pit the moral power of judicial reason against the physical power of armed force, by subjecting international violence to impartial factual determination and legal judgment.

Dispensation from factual determination and legal judgment in our society is an indulgence reserved for protecting governments from loss of face. For them there is an understood rule of sovereign immunity.[11] When governments play at violence, law takes a holiday. When governments loot and kill, law looks the other way.

The present proposal is to change the rule, to replace the security of judicial immunity with the risks of exposure and censure, to replace indulgence with accountability. The proposal is offered in the belief that when sovereign immunity is tempered, the game of violence will be moderated by some measure of deterrence.

Sovereignty may seem undeterrable. It is not invulnerable. Its point of vulnerability is precisely the fear of losing face. This is the point at which the pressure of impartial judgment would be felt. This is the respect in which nations may be more amenable to legal control than individuals. This is the place of opportunity for deterrence, the opportunity that could be seized by an International Peace Court.

[11] A classic enunciation of the rule of sovereign immunity is that of a national tribunal, the United States Supreme Court, in *The Schooner Exchange v. McFaddon*, 7 Cranch 116 (1812). The issue was whether a public armed vessel of France which had come into the port of Philadelphia could be subjected to the power of the United States District Court. The American plaintiffs claimed ownership, alleging that the ship had been seized in 1810 on the high seas by agents of the French Emperor. In affirming the District Court's dismissal, the Supreme Court reasoned in the words of Chief Justice John Marshall:

> One sovereign being in no respect amenable to another, and being bound by obligations of the highest character not to degrade the dignity of his nation, by placing himself or its sovereign rights within the jurisdiction of another, can be supposed to enter a foreign territory only under an express license, or in the confidence that the immunities belonging to his independent sovereign station, though not expressly stipulated, are reserved by implication, and will be extended to him.

The rule of sovereign immunity is honored by international tribunals. Their custom is not to entertain actions against unconsenting national governments as party defendants.

INTERNATIONAL VIOLENCE: THE TOTAL CHALLENGE AND THE PARTIAL RESPONSE

International Violence: The Total Challenge

The meaning of international violence in a nuclear age is that it brings mankind face to face with the total challenge. "... a world war in this day and age," according to British Marshal, Sir John Slessor, "would be general suicide and the end of civilization as we know it."[1] A full-scale nuclear exchange lasting less than sixty minutes, according to President John F. Kennedy, could kill 300 million people and leave the environment so devastated that the survivors would envy the dead.[2]

But the challenge is not limited to nuclear threat in the ultimacy of war. It includes the assault upon the quality of human life posed, for example, by radioactive fallout from experimental nuclear explosions.[3] One expert testified in the 1963 hearings of the Foreign Relations Committee of the United States Senate, for example, that 50,000 children would be born with defects such as muscular dystrophy, blindness and dwarfism as a result of the nuclear testing that had already taken place.[4]

Nor can the challenge be gauged on the international scale alone. It has to be measured as well by its impact on domestic programs of social necessity placed in default by the massive diversion of resources to the military priority. It has to be measured by what it does to the starving children of an underpriviledged African state engulfed in a war of independence.[5] It has to be measured by what it does to even a

[1] In Hart, *Deterrent or Defense* 22 (1960). For the effects of a nuclear attack, see generally Stonier, *Nuclear Disaster* (1963).

[2] *Public Papers of the Presidents: John F. Kennedy*, 1963, p. 603 (1964).

[3] See Reports of the U. N. Scientific Committee on the Effects of Atomic Radiation, of June 13, 1958 and March 23, 1962, Gen. Assembly, *Off. Rec., Thirteenth Sess. Supp. No. 17* (A/3838) pp. 36–43, and *Off. Rec., Seventeenth Sess. Supp. No. 16* (A/5216) pp. 31–35.

[4] U. S. Senate, For. Rels. Comm., 88th Cong., 1st Sess., *Nuclear Test Ban Hearings* 949 (1963).

[5] See "Africa – Hunger As A Political Weapon in Nigeria," *N.Y. Times* July 7, 1968, p. E3: "... 13,000 dying daily now, according to the International Red Cross, perhaps two million dead within two months ...." The reality of the statistics in this conflict between

materially favored nation, such as the United States, which, despite an impoverished sector of thirty million people,[6] feels itself obliged to divert over seventy billion dollars a year to a military budget.[7]

It is not just the basic necessities of national life that are made to pay for the war system, however. The higher needs are also preempted. President Lyndon B. Johnson drew a graphic vignette of the impact of the military preemption upon higher education. He said that: "The cost of acquiring and maintaining one squadron of supersonic aircraft diverts resources that would build and maintain a university."[8]

Very simply, the challenge of international violence is critical to national life as well as to international life. Indeed, the maintenance of the inclusive order of the international community has become nothing less than a pre-condition to the adequate maintenance of the particular order of each country's domestic community.

The Partial Response

The world community's reply to international violence has been less than commensurate with the magnitude of the challenge. There has been a partial response, however, consisting of both general blueprints and limited collective decisions for the systematic control of violence.

The Security Council

Foremost among the general blueprints[9] is the United Nations Charter, which replaced the Covenant of the League of Nations in 1945 as the world community's most authoritative proscription of violence. The Charter further provided the implementation of a control mechanism built around the primary responsibility of a Security Council:

> In order to ensure prompt and effective action by the United Nations, its Members confer on the Security Council primary responsibility for the maintenance of international peace and security, and agree that in carrying out its duties under this responsibility the Security Council acts on their behalf.[10]

Nigeria and Biafra is suggested by Robison, "The Children of Biafra," *ibid.:*

> Father Sean Guino, a tall 40-year-old Irish Priest, told of his walk around the mission wards seven days before: "Four little children were lying on a bed. One was dead and I couldn't notice the difference. I saw a child suckling her mother's breast and the mother was dead."

[6] See *U. S. News and World Report*, May 13, 1968, p. 48; see further, generally, Harrington, *The Other America* (1962).

[7] Exec. Off. of the President/Bur. of the Budget, *The Budget In Brief* 14–15 (1969).

[8] Eighteen Nation Disarmament Committee (hereinafter cited ENDC) PV 235, Jan. 27, 1966, p. 23.

[9] For a historical survey of formulations of plans for the maintenance of peace among nations, see McDougal and Feliciano, *Law and Minimum World Public Order* 263–66 (1961).

[10] U. N. Charter, Art. 24.

The Security Council was expected to discharge its primary responsibility by making determinations of peace violations and deciding upon appropriate responses including resort, when necessary, to economic and military measures:

> The Security Council shall determine the existence of any threat to the peace, breach of the peace, or act of aggression and shall make recommendations, or decide what measures shall be taken in accordance with Articles 41 and 42, to maintain or restore international peace and security.[11]

The Council contains fifteen members, ten of which are temporary and five permanent:[12] the United States, the Soviet Union, the United Kingdom, France and China.[13] The exercise of the Council's primary responsibility for the maintenance of international peace and security, it should be noted, is subjected by the Charter to a requirement of unanimity among these five.[14]

The Collective Decisions

Much of the response to the problem of international violence has taken place outside the framework of the Security Council in collective decisions directed to limited sectors of the problem: notably to the menace of the nuclear weapons capability held by the United States, the United Kingdom, the Soviet Union, France and the Peoples' Republic of China, and to the threat posed by the prospect of its spread to many other nations. It has been estimated that at least ten of the non-nuclear states either had or soon would have, the ability to make atomic weapons: West Germany, India, Japan, Belgium, Canada, Czechoslovakia, Israel, Italy, the Netherlands, and Sweden.[15] These collective decisions include:

1. The Nuclear Test Ban Treaty, which orginated in an agreement at Moscow on August 5, 1963, by the United States, the United Kingdom and the Soviet Union, and which was ratified for the United States by President Kennedy on October 7, 1963,[16] and went into force

[11] *Id.*, Art. 39. Articles 41 and 42 are set forth *infra*, Chapter IV.
[12] *Id.*, Art. 23 as amended.
[13] *Ibid.*
[14] *Id.*, Art. 27 as amended.
[15] See *U. S. News and World Report*, July 18, 1966, p. 52.
[16] Treaty Banning Nuclear Weapon Tests In The Atmosphere, In Outer Space And Under Water, 14 *United States Treaties* 1313; *Treaties and Other International Acts Series* (hereinafter cited TIAS) 5433; 480 *United Nations Treaty Series* (hereinafter cited UNTS) 43. For a commentary see Schwelb, "The Nuclear Test Ban Treaty and International Law," 58 *American Journal of International Law* 643 (1964).

on October 10, 1963 with the participation of some one hundred two signatory states;[17]

2. The United Nations General Assembly resolution prohibiting the orbiting of weapons of mass destruction,[18] followed by the Treaty on Principles Governing the Activities of States in the Exploration and Use of Outer Space, Including the Moon and Other Celestial Bodies, which prohibited the orbiting or stationing of nuclear arms or weapons of mass destruction in outer space, which was approved by the United Nations Committee On The Peaceful Use Of Outer Space on December 8, 1966;[19] and after signature and ratification entered into force for the United States October 10, 1967;[20] and

3. The Treaty on The Non-proliferation Of Nuclear Weapons which was negotiated in the Eighteen Nation Disarmament Conference, endorsed by the General Assembly, and opened for signature on July 1, 1968.[21]

The Response Appraised

The level of expectation which launched the Security Council has not been matched by the level of its performance. Despite instances of unequivocal response to peace infractions,[22] the record is one of sub-

[17] See TIAS 5433 at 16–17.

[18] General Assembly Resolution 1884 (XVIII).

[19] *N. Y. Times*, Dec. 9, 1966, pp. 1 and 18.

[20] TIAS 6347. Article 4 of the treaty reads:

> States parties to the treaty undertake not to place in orbit around the earth any objects carrying nuclear weapons or any other kinds of weapons of mass destruction, install such weapons on celestial bodies, or station such weapons in outer space in any other manner.

[21] U. N. Doc. A/7016/ADD. 1; see *N. Y. Times*, May 2, 1968, p. 12, June 11, 1968, pp. 1, 3, July 2, 1968, pp. 1, 3: *U. S. State Dept. Bulletin*, July 22, 1968, p. 85. Article 1 of the treaty reads:

> Each nuclear-weapon State Party to the Treaty undertakes not to transfer to any recipient whatsoever nuclear weapons or other nuclear explosive devices or control over such weapons or explosive devices directly, or indirectly; and not in any way to assist, encourage, or induce any non-nuclear-weapon State to manufacture or otherwise acquire nuclear weapons or other nuclear explosive devices, or control over such weapons or explosive devices.

For a commentary see Willrich, *Non-Proliferation Treaty: Framework for Nuclear Arms Control* (1969).

[22] See, e.g., the following Security Council Resolutions:

Resolution S/902; Security Council, *Off. Rec., III, Supp.* for *July, 1948*, in which the Security Council:

> Determines that the situation in Palestine constitutes a threat to the peace within the meaning of Article 39 of the Charter; ...
> Orders ... an immediate and unconditional cease fire ....

Resolution S/1501, S. C., *Off. Rec., V, Resolutions and Decisions, 1950* (S/INF 5/Rev. 1), in which the Security Council:

> Noting with grave concern the armed attack upon the Republic of Korea by forces from North Korea, Determines that this action constitutes a breach of the peace ...

stantial default in the discharge of its primary responsibility in the face of dire community need, as seen in the case of the conflict in Vietnam.[23] This default stems from the absence among the permanent members of that unanimity which was presupposed in the United Nations Charter as a condition for the exercise of the Security Council's power.[24]

Meanwhile the toll of violence mounts:

> There have been some fifty military conflicts that could be graced by the name of war since 1945, sixteen of them fought between sovereign nations, the others anti-colonial or anti-governmental uprisings, twenty of these with foreign troops involved. Eleven of these conflicts were of such a nature that they threatened global peace, but far outnumbering the major cases have been the outbreaks of local violence, some of them almost unnoticed by the world at large but where, in some, the dead were counted in the hundred of thousands.[25]

The three treaties, while effective to some degree, are only a partial community reaction to the problem of violence.

The Nuclear Test Ban Treaty has successfully inhibited its signatories from testing in air, space and water,[26] but not under ground. It is also a potential brake on nuclear proliferation in that testing may be a necessary condition for the development of nuclear-weapon capabilities,[27] for without the ability to test as a means of quality control the motive for nuclear weapon production would be reduced.[28]

However, the test ban has not stopped testing by the two nuclear states which have not subscribed to it, France and mainland China.[29]

[23] See, e.g., Middleton, "U. N. Crisis of Confidence," *N. Y. Times*, Sept. 25, 1967, p. 2, quoting Torsten L. Nilsson, Foreign Minister of Sweden, thus:

> Situations which undoubtedly constitute threats to the peace or breaches of the peace – even a major war as the one in Vietnam – can continue for years without any United Nations intervention at all.

[24] See Middleton, *ibid.*:

> In the opinion of most senior members of the permanent Secretariat and representatives of the smaller nations, the impotence of the United Nations in dealing with crises is the result, primarily of the rivalry between the United States and the Soviet Union.

[25] C. and S. Mydans, *The Violent Peace* 4–5 (1968).

[26] Article 1 reads in part as follows:

> Each of the parties to this Treaty undertakes to prohibit, to prevent, and not to carry out any nuclear weapon test explosion, or any other nuclear explosion, at any place under its jurisdiction or control:
> (a) in the atmosphere; beyond its limits, including outer space; or under water, including territorial waters or high seas; or
> (b) in any other environment if such explosion causes radioactive debris to be present outside the territorial limits of the State under whose jurisdiction or control such explosion is conducted.

[27] See, e.g., Brennan and Halperin, "Policy Considerations of a Nuclear Test Ban," in Brennan (ed.) *Arms Control, Disarmament and National Security*, 244 (1961).

[28] *Id.*, at 241.

[29] See, e.g., *N. Y. Times*, July 8, 1968, p. 7:

> French scientists exploded the conventional atomic warhead ... in the Tuamotu Archipelago ....
> It was the 10th nuclear test at the proving grounds. Six were held in 1966 and three in

The purpose of the ban on the orbiting of weapons in space can be circumvented by sending armed missiles on a sub-orbital route.[30]

And the non-proliferation treaty is vulnerable to defeasance by non-compliance, and weakened by the limited ability of signatory nuclear states to guarantee to a non-nuclear state adequate security against nuclear menace by a nonsignatory nuclear state.

While there has been headway, therefore, toward the protection of the community from atomic violence, the community response so far has been partial. Moreover, it has resulted in raised expectations which express themselves in a crescendo of demands for complete protection.

These demands surfaced in a General Assembly resolution in 1963,[31] which noted that the preamble to the Nuclear Test Ban Treaty proclaims the intention of the parties to achieve a ban on all test explosions, even those underground, and requested the Eighteen Nation Committee to move forward to this full objective. They were channeled through a General Assembly resolution in 1968, which commended the Treaty on the Non-proliferation of Nuclear Weapons, and urged the Committee and the nuclear states to seek the end of the nuclear arms race as well as nuclear disarmament and general disarmament under strict and effective international control.[32]

But the impetus of commingled rising expectation and sense of frustration has been especially heard in the voices of the non-nuclear states raised in the deliberations of the Eighteen Nation Committee. Among these is the voice of the eight non-nuclear members of the Conference (Brazil, Burma, Ethiopia, India, Mexico, Nigeria, Sweden and the United Arab Republic) which objected to reliance on mere partial measures:

> The eight delegations are convinced that measures to prohibit the spread of nuclear weapons should, therefore, be coupled with or followed by tangible steps to halt the nuclear arms race and to limit, reduce, and eliminate the stocks of nuclear weapons and the means of their delivery.[33]

The voice of Representative Imru of Ethiopia reechoed the demand

1967.

See further *N. Y. Times*, Aug. 25, 1968, p. 1, reporting the first French thermonuclear blast, Aug. 24, 1968. See *U. S. News and World Report*, July 25, 1966, p. 43 on mainland China's nuclear detonations.

[30] See Clark, "New Offensive Weapons of U. S. and Soviet Imperil Treaty's Plan to Keep Space Free of War," *N. Y. Times*, Dec. 26, 1967, p. 23.

[31] General Assembly Resolution 1910 (XVIII).

[32] General Assembly Resolution 2373 (XXII).

[33] Conference Of The Eighteen Nation Committee On Disarmament, 158, Sept. 15, 1965, p. 18.

for the end of the nuclear arms race in protection of the interests of all peoples:

The partial test-ban Treaty may safeguard the interests of a few big Powers; but since it has not halted the nuclear arms race it cannot be said to protect the interests of all nations and peoples. It has even enabled the nuclear Powers to diversify and perfect their nuclear weapons by undertaking tests without protest from the peoples of the world.[34]

But even the extension of the nuclear test ban to underground explosions could not be a total answer to the demands which the anxiety of the non-nuclear states is communicating to the nuclear states, as voiced by Mrs. Myrdal, the Swedish representative:

As for the nuclear powers, a complete test ban might only deprive them of some prospects of further perfecting their nuclear weapons – that is, make more stable a situation which is at present dangerously dynamic and which would continue to be dynamic, even under a non-proliferation treaty... It is this dynamic aspect of the present gap that weighs heavily with the non-nuclear Powers.[35]

An effective summing up of these expectations was provided by the representative of India, Mr. Trivedi:

No international treaty can, therefore, be acceptable which issues dictates only to non-nuclear countries not to do this or that, particularly when the countries possessing nuclear weapons do not assume any prior commitments themselves.[36]

Through these voices the non-nuclear members of the world community are demanding of the nuclear states an exercise of responsibility that goes beyond tokenism and partial gestures. They are saying that they want an adequate response to the deathly condition of the world body politic, not band-aid treatment.

[34] ENDC, PV 229, Sept. 2, 1965, p. 15.
[35] ENDC, PV 222, Aug. 10, 1965, p. 17.
[36] ENDC, PV 223, Aug. 12, 1965, p. 15.

III

MISSION: A MOVE TOWARD LAW

The Exercise of Responsibility

Our response obviously falls short of our responsibility. Adlai Stevenson measured our responsibility for meeting the challenge of violence at the international level by our responsibility at the national level:

> At home we live under law. We play our part in promoting the general welfare. We share some sense of national purpose. These are surely the minimum conditions of a truly civic life, or a life in society that deserves the name of human.
>
> But all are lacking in our international world. Should not, therefore, the introduction of such fundamental institutions be the first aim of world policy?[1]

The first question of world policy is the exercise of the responsibility for peace. Shall it be by the few or by the many?

By The Few

The primary responsibility was granted to the five great powers: the United States, the Soviet Union, the United Kingdom, France and China. To these the general community of nations has given permanent seats and substantive vetos in the Security Council. And to the Security Council itself has been given "primary responsibility for the maintenance of international peace and security" with the understanding that "in carrying out its duties under this responsibility the Security Council acts on their behalf."

Now, for the exercise of a responsibility of this magnitude, one would expect to see a mobilization of moral and physical resources in total commitment to the priority of the rule of law in the world. But evidently no such priority has been assigned by these major trustees of peace and security to their own foreign policies. The pursuit of separate interests still comes first, the inclusive interest[2] in international order second.

[1] Stevenson, "Full Promise of a Distracted World," in Cleveland (ed.) *The Promise of World Tensions* 128 (1961).

[2] Cf. McDougal, Lasswell and Vlasic, *Law and Public Order In Space* 157 (1963):

The paradox is that this situation is justified in the name of security.

Not only have the great powers in the Security Council been ineffective in discharging their primary responsibility for international peace and security when confronted by open violence as in Vietnam, they have even compounded their failure by actively supporting opposite sides. The ideological battleline that divides them among themselves has even divided one of them within itself, that being China.

By The Many

The non-discharge of responsibility by the few, however, does not mean its abandonment by everyone else. If the initiative for world law is not claimed by its primary grantees, it may be reclaimed by its grantors. The rescue indeed seems to be taking shape. The old acquiescence of the many in the initiative of the few is changing. Instead of waiting in silence for the great powers to make up their minds, to decide what is good for all, the voices of many lesser powers are being heard speaking their own minds, asserting their own claim to share in the process of global decision, and exercising a new found initiative. In particular, the sound of a new surge of responsibility for peace and security is heard from the voices of the non-nuclear nations which have been participating in the global town-meeting of the Eighteen Nation Disarmament Committee, the now enlarged forum which hammered out the Nuclear Non-proliferation Treaty. What these voices seem to be saying to the nuclear powers is that the exercise of responsibility for global law is not going to be permitted to fail through the default of the few; it is going to be shared by the many. The message is voiced in the following accents:

From the voice of Mr. Azeredo da Silveira of Brazil –

For such is the kind of treaty to which we are looking forward: not a text agreed privately between the super-Powers and destined to passive accession by the rest of the nations....[3]

From the voice of Mr. Burns of Canada –

> We emphasize the enormous importance of giving full recognition to inclusive interests, since the present perilous state of the world arena is the result of inadequate awareness of the inclusivity of effects (interdeterminations) and of insufficient action to bring institutions into line with the manifest needs of the situation.

These authors define inclusive interests, at p. 151, as:

> ... the demands and expectations that affect collective processes to a significant degree, and therefore justify procedures that bring more than a single nation-state into the control of the process.

[3] ENDC, PV 310, July 4, 1967, p. 5.

...we have all made it clear that there should be reciprocal obligations of the nuclear powers and the States not possessing nuclear weapons.[4]

From the voice of Mr. Obi of Nigeria –

A universal approach to the problem is not only essential but desirable and inescapable. After all, the treaty on non-proliferation, should we achieve one, would impose heavier obligations on the non-nuclear Powers than on the nuclear Powers.[5]

From the voice of Mr. Correa da Costa of Brazil –

At the start the main obstacle was the lack of agreement between the two super-Powers; today there are auspicious signs that a basic agreement is in the process of being reached. It remains now to bring it into line with the legitimate interests of the non-nuclear-weapon countries of the world.[6]

From these voices – no sound of subservience to major power interests. Only the sound of insistence upon universally shared responsibility on behalf of the common interests is heard.

Mission: A Move Toward World Law

This sharing of responsibility by the smaller powers is a natural sequel to the default of consensus of the major powers in responding to the challenge of violence. However, if this broader based responsibility is to be effectively exercised, it must itself be supported by a consensus around a common objective tailored to the capabilities of the lesser nations. To them must be given a specific mission.

Obviously their mission cannot be that which is specific to the permanent members of the Security Council, who, in effect, were expected to provide a world legal system for peace organized around their superior military, economic and diplomatic competence,[7] a system to be complemented with contributions from the other United Nations Members.[8] (Pending the organization of these national contributions through

[4] ENDC, PV 306, June 20, 1967, p. 4.

[5] ENDC, PV 235, Jan. 27, 1966, p. 30.

[6] ENDC, PV 297, May 18, 1967, p. 14.

[7] It was the declared expectation of their own responsibilities in support of Council decisions relating to the maintenance of peace and security that was said, by the permanent Members, to justify their veetos. See "Statement by the delegations of the four sponsoring Governments on voting procedure in the Security Council," in II *Repertory of Practice of United Nations Organs*, Annex IV, pp. 104–06 (1955), and, in particular, at Part I, para. 9:

> In view of the primary responsibilities of the permanent members, they could not be expected, in the present condition of the world, to assume the obligation to act in so serious a matter as the maintenance of international peace and security in consequence of a decision in which they had not concurred.

[8] U. N. Charter, Arts. 41–50.

agreements required by the Charter,[9] moreover, the nucleus of five nations was given authority for an interim regulatory system.[10])

The mission of the many nations cannot be to assemble the elaborate system assigned by the Charter to the five great powers. But it can be to invent a move toward a future legal order by simply taking a first step toward the deterrence of violence. It is not necessary to know exactly what steps will follow, or by what path they will lead someday to a world law of peace. From the vantage of the first step taken, it will be possible to sight the direction of the next step to be taken. Any move away from disorder is a move toward law.

A move toward world law is proposed, therefore, as a realistic mission for the nations which are becoming increasingly responsive to the challenge of international violence. The mission is not to prescribe the substance of a world legal order for the control of violence, but to start the procedure which can be expected to lead to it.

For acceptance, it should not be necessary that the prospectus of this procedure chart its future course of development. It is necessary, however, that the prospectus demonstrate a potential for effectiveness and for legitimacy.

Credentials of Acceptability: Effectiveness and Legitimacy

The acceptability of any enterprise of common responsibility, however ideal, would be compromised by a failure to exhibit a convincing potential for effectiveness. The promise of effectiveness is required, be-

[9] Article 43.

1. All Members of the United Nations, in order to contribute to the maintenance of international peace and security, undertake to make available to the Security Council, on its call and in accordance with a special agreement or agreements, armed forces, assistance, and facilities, including rights of passage, necessary for the purpose of maintaining international peace and security.

2. Such agreement or agreements shall govern the numbers and types of forces, their degree of readiness and general location, and the nature of the facilities and assistance to be provided.

3. The agreement or agreements shall be negotiated as soon as possible on the initiative of the Security Council. They shall be concluded between the Security Council and Members or between the Security Council and groups of Members and shall be subject to ratification by the signatory states in accordance with their respective constitutional processes.

[10] Article 106.

Pending the coming into force of such special agreements referred to in Article 43 as in the opinion of the Security Council enable it to begin the exercise of its responsibilities under Article 42, the parties to the Four-Nation Declaration, signed at Moscow, October 30, 1943, and France, shall, in accordance with the provisions of paragraph 5 of that Declaration, consult with one another and as occasion requires with other Members of the United Nations with a view to such joint action on behalf of the Organization as may be necessary for the purpose of maintaining international peace and security.

cause idealism cannot be expected to attract support unless it is conjoined with practicality. Effectiveness in this instance may have to be assembled, if not from the unanimity and resources of all the permanent members of the Security Council, from the shared objectives and shared resources of the larger community of nations.

Acceptance would equally be compromised by illegitimacy, that is, by the failure to respect the other basic values evolving through international expectations as expressed in legal norms. Legitimacy is essential to the holding of long-run plans.[11] The enterprise must be legal.

Summary

The exercise of responsibility for the promotion of a world order of peace and security is shifting from the few major powers to the larger community of nations.

The immediate mission proposed for the new initiative is to find an effective legal procedure for a move toward world law.

The stalemate of consensus at the upper level of the international structure indicates that if the move is going to be made, and if the requirements of effectiveness and legitimacy are going to be met, the community must proceed through reliance upon factors of resource and authority which are available at a lower base of international consensus.

The design may begin with an inventory of these factors.

[11] Cf. the explanation of the requirement of legitimacy in Deutsch, "The Commitment of National Legitimacy Symbols as a Verification Technique," VIII *The Journal of Conflict Resolution* 360–64 (1963) and I *The Journal of Arms Control* 454–59 (1963), notably at 360–61 and 454–55 respectively:

> Legitimacy is the assurance of the compatibility of a value-pursuing course of action with other key values, and hence with the maintenance of the personality system of the actor ....
>
> This view implies that legitimacy is essential to the functioning of a system. It is the assurance to persons acting in the system that in acting in accordance with one of their roles, or pursuing one of their values, they will not destroy other vital roles or other major values.

IV

MEDIUM: AN INTERNATIONAL PEACE COURT

The Choice of Means

What then are the significant resources that the international community can marshal in organizing somewhere below the level of the Security Council for the control of violence?

The Traditional Instruments of Power

The traditional catalogue of resources available for the effectuation of international policy has stressed military, economic, and diplomatic power. Examples are the measures which the United Nations Charter makes available for authorization by the Security Council. Article 41 provides for economic and diplomatic measures:

> These may include complete or partial interruption of economic relations and of rail, sea, postal, telegraphic, radio, and other means of communication, and the severance of diplomatic relations.

Article 42 provides for military measures:

> Should the Security Council consider that measures provided for in Article 41 would be inadequate or have proved to be inadequate, it may take such action by air, sea, or land forces as may be necessary to maintain or restore international peace and security. Such action may include demonstrations, blockade, and other operations by air, sea, or land forces of Members of the United Nations.

Whatever may have been their merits in the past, and however comfortable it may be to think of continuing to rely upon them, these familiar instruments of international power have become associated with certain disabilities which compromise their acceptability as future instruments of legal deterrence.

Military

One disadvantage of the military instrument lies in its obvious ambivalence of effect. Its tendency to regulate and control violence is offset by an equal and opposite tendency to stimulate not only the violence of reprisal but that loss of control which is signalled by escalation. This feature is amply documented in the Vietnamese conflict.

The military instrument is beset by the further obvious disadvantage of cost in lives, health, homes, and money, again as evidenced by Vietnam.

Ambivalent effect and prohibitive cost, accordingly, combine to compromise the prospect of performance of the military resource as a deterrent instrument. If applied as a sanction against one of the major armed powers, military measures would be just another name for war itself.

The ultimate *reductio ad absurdum* of reliance upon the military instrument is the paradox depicted by Professor Gerhart Niemeyer:

> ...an international order which depends on force as its *ultima ratio* is a permanent source of international struggle rather than a medium of order.[1]

Economic

Parallel comment may be applied to the instrument of economic pressure. Its potential too is qualified by factors of ambivalence and cost. Severe economic sanctioning measures run the danger of provoking violent retaliation.[2] Short of retaliation, their effectiveness may be compromised by the target state's resort to internal defenses such as stockpiling, rationing, and the development of substitute materials,[3] as well as by external defenses such as new trade outlets, new sources, and credit offered by sympathizers.[4] Thus the application of economic pressure runs the risk of being counterproductive. For example, the economic sanctions imposed by the Security Council against Rhodesia have been followed by Rhodesia's cutback of imports, diversification of agriculture and opening of new mining operations.[5]

[1] Niemeyer, *Law Without Force, The Function Of Politics In International Law* 21–22 (1941). Cf. McDougal, Lasswell and Vlasic, *Law And Public Order In Space* 158 (1963):

> An essential connotation of minimum order is that it will be possible to maintain it short of great destructive measures of enforcement. No genuine public order exists if it is necessary from time to time to fight a civil war as a means of vindicating control and authority.

Cf. Borchard, "The 'Enforcement' Of Peace By 'Sanctions,'" 27 *American Journal Of International Law* 524 (1933):

> To engender peace by the threat of force is inherently incongruous, for it arouses, when applied to groups, fear and resentment.

[2] See, e.g., Taubenfeld and Taubenfeld, "The 'Economic Weapon': The League and the United Nations," *Proc. Am. Soc. Int. Law, Fifty-Eighth Annual Mtg. April 23–25, 1964*, p. 201.

[3] See U. N. Collective Measures Committee, "Report," in General Assembly, *Off. Rec., Sixth Session, Supp. No. 13* (A/1891) p. 7, section 49 (1951).

[4] See Taubenfeld, *op. cit.*, at 193.

[5] See Fellows, "Life in Rhodesia Is Little Changed – U. N. Curbs Have Brought Few Signs Of Discomfort," *N. Y. Times*, June 30, 1968, p. 13.

A highly developed state may be relatively immune to economic measures by reason of economic independence resting on the possession of its own food resources, an adequate complement of raw materials, and its own scientific and technical resources.[6]

Moreover, the cost of administering economic measures may be severe. The sanctioner himself may suffer from the consequences of disrupted relations with the sanctioned. A sanctioned state may owe money on foreign claims which creditor nations would obviously jeopardize if they were to sever trade relations with it pursuant to an international sanctioning program.[7]

The problems associated with the application of the economic instrument have been summarized by the Collective Measures Committee of the United Nations:

> The economic problems with which some nations are confronted when called upon to sever trade vital to their economies - problems, among others, of maintaining the living standards of their people – are serious. The provision of assistance may result in a substantial charge upon the resources of the Member nations. The possibility of reprisal, either through counter-economic measures or by force, must also be recognized.[8]

Diplomatic

Diplomatic discourse can be a vital instrument of peace. However, diplomatic pressure may be deployed in various forms, such as the withholding of recognition from a state or its government, or the severance of diplomatic relations, or the denial of association with the United Nations,[9] and may have disruptive repercussions in the community, even affecting the states which apply the measures. By way of practical example the Collective Measures Committee warns that:

> The matter of non-recognition is bound to raise a great number of questions in a concrete case, for instance, with regard to participation in international conventions or international agencies, postal service, currency, passports, consulates, immigration quotas, custom treatment, public debt, public property abroad, extradition, citizenship, mining concessions, etc.[10]

In view of the severe structures on the use of the modern military resource and because of the serious problems associated with the use of the economic and diplomatic pressures, it may be reasonable to anticipate that national leaderships concerned with the problem of de-

[6] See *supra* note 3, p. 7, section 47.
[7] See *id.*, p. 12, section 93.
[8] See *id.*, p. 20, section 162.
[9] See *id.*, pp. 5–6, sections 38, 39.
[10] *Ibid.*, section 39.

terring international violence will be predisposed to explore the use of an alternative instrument in an effort to design an organized international response to the problem of violence.

A New Instrument: The Power of Mass Communication

An alternative instrument is available. The traditional military, economic and diplomatic resources are not the only or necessarily the most appropriate base of international leverage. Through the development of electronic communication, an alternative instrument of influence has been placed at the disposal of the community of nations, an instrument that is new and distinctive, one that can compete with the other instruments both in operation and in accessibility.

The military and economic instruments both exploit and are bound by material power, but electronic communication overcomes the old bounds of matter and taps the power of ideas and moral sentiment.

The diplomatic instrument facilitates communications to governments, but electronics makes possible instant and pervasive communications not just to governments but to entire populations.[11]

The distribution of military and economic assets is significantly weighted in favor of a few nations, but access to electronic communication is significantly spread among all the nations.

The capacity so to transcend the conventional bounds of nature and the traditional lines of asset distribution equips the electronic instrument with an open-ended potential for influencing mass attitudes and responses in the international community.[12]

[11] Cf. the reference by McDougal and Feliciano to ideological strategies, which – "relate principally to the selection of symbols to be circulated in the target audience and to the establishment and maintenance of centers and channels of communication through which the symbols chosen are put into circulation." *Law and Minimum World Public Order* 317 (1961). "Ideological strategy is oriented toward the influencing of the attitudes of large groups." *Ibid.*

[12] Cf. Marks, "Peacekeeping And The Settlement Of International Disputes," in World Peace Through Law Center, *World Peace Through Law, The Geneva Conference* 95 (1969):

> The Communications Revolution in our century – and most particularly in the last ten years – has been of such a startling magnitude that perhaps the thorniest intellectual problem of our era is to foresee and plan for its almost limitless consequences .... Harnessing steam made it possible to link human muscle to machinery, and to greatly amplify the mechanical output. Harnessing the electron makes it possible to link billions of human minds together, and to multiply manyfold the mental output.
>
> ... What characterizes our era from all the countless millennia that have preceded it is precisely this: it is now feasible to bring millions, and even billions, of human minds to bear on the same piece of data – and to do so simultaneously.
>
> In essence, we are in the process of achieving through *technology* what every religion, every ideology, every credo has dreamed of doing: uniting the masses of mankind for common goals.

The Choice of Method

The new instrument of communication can be applied to deterrence in different ways. Two important methods of application are available: the appeal, for use before violence occurs, and the censure, for use after it occurs. Both methods have an observed capacity to exert influence upon the subjectivities of governments.

Appeals

It is axiomatic that the pen is mightier than the sword. Just so, the communication of appeals, when peace is imperiled, may be mightier than gunpowder. Professor Niemeyer explained the principle:

An appeal is a psychological reality. It can be observed and analyzed with relative accuracy. It is no less a reality and no less an empirical fact than the action of gunpowder or the convincing argument which lies in the point of a bayonet.[13]

Part of the reality of an appeal is the amplitude of its impact. Through the electronic media the message is carried not just to the menacing government but to the whole community. The Collective Measures Committee of the United Nations has confirmed the pervasive influence of appeals deployed by the Security Council and the General Assembly in these words:

Though primarily addressed to the parties these appeals also drew the attention of other nations to a possible or actual threat to or breach of the peace, Such appeals . . . may contribute to inform public opinion and to mobilize it in support of United States action.[14]

Censure

The appeal, however, is not the only or necessarily the most appropriate adaptation of the communication instrument to deterrence. If, as indicated by the Collective Measures Committee, public appeals may serve to inform and mobilize public opinion in support of community reaction to violence, it is submitted that public censure will make an even stronger impression on public opinion and that the

[13] Niemeyer, *op. cit. supra* at 22.

[14] See *supra* note 3, p. 5, section 38. By appeals the Committee means:
Appeals to parties, such as:
(I) Appeals to settle their dispute by peaceful means;
(II) Appeals to settle their dispute by specific method;
(III) Appeals to refrain or desist from activities in violation of the Charter, liable to lead to a threat to the peace;
(IV) Appeals to comply with specific provisional measures in the case of a threat to the peace, breach of the peace or act of aggression. *Ibid.*

consequent impact of public opinion on governmental subjectivities will be correspondingly greater.

Censure is the method, therefore, which will be developed as a deterrent strategy in the present proposal.

A profound sensitivity on the part of states and governments to any public imputation of illegal conduct has been observed by respected investigators in international law.

The finding of J. L. Brierly is that:

...a state knows that a breach of International Law rarely fails to be notorious; and... every state is extraordinarily sensitive to the mere suspicion of illegal action.[15]

Roger Fisher has explained that:

A government is concerned not only with what the party most directly affected by the breach of a rule might do, it is also concerned with the effect of the breach on others. In the international sphere, this concern is usually with what is called "world public opinion."[16]

The deterrent capability of the censure is postulated upon the impact of its anticipation upon the sensitivities of the government which contemplates wrongdoing. The deterrent power of the anticipated disapproval of international public opinion has been underlined by Howard and Rita Taubenfeld:

In fact, experience shows that publicity and the threat of international disapproval may be effective in preventing an international dispute from becoming a breach of the peace or an aggression, even in a world of iron curtains and sophisticated propaganda machinery.[17]

The great practitioner of international relations, United States Secretary of State Elihu Root, attested to the influence of general opinion upon even the most powerful governments from:

a consciousness that in the most important affairs of nations, in their political status, the success of their undertakings and their process of development, there is an indefinite and almost mysterious influence exercised by the general opinion

[15] Brierly, "Sanctions," 17 *Transactions Of The Grotius Society* 69–70 (1932).

[16] Fisher, "Constructing Rules That Affect Governments," in Brennan (ed.) *Arms Control, Disarmament and National Security* 58 (1961). See further *ibid.*:

> ... in some circumstances the views of third states may be more feared than retaliatory action. Presumably the Soviet decision to respect the rule of non-intervention in the Congo was brought about in significant part by concern for the views of third states. In a world in which actions speak louder than words, governments which engage in propaganda weigh the effect of their actions on third states.

[17] Taubenfeld, *op. cit.*, at 204. Compare Cahn and Cahn, "The New Sovereign Immunity," 81 *Harvard Law Review* 929, 936–7 (1968), thus:

> ... the mere threat of exposure in a neutral forum would have a singularly salutary impact on the execution of an administrator's duties.

of the world regarding the nation's character and conduct. The greatest and strongest governments recognize this influence and act with reference to it. . . .[18]

Evidence of governmental sensitivity to the power of public opinion was left in the wake of the invasion of Czechoslovakia by Soviet troops on August 20, 1968. Raymond H. Anderson wrote the following report on the Soviet reaction to the nearly universal denunciation of this act of violence:

A worried tone over the crisis in Czechoslovakia emerged in Soviet commentaries today after several days of confident assertion of the justice of the invasion.

A worldwide outcry of condemnation, especially from other Communist parties, has apparently unsettled the Soviet leadership.[19]

Further evidence tending to show the sensitivity of state governments to public denunciation is available in the experience of the European Court of Justice, the judicial organ serving the three separate regional communities: the European Economic Community, the European Coal and Steel Community, and the European Atomic Energy Community. (The six member states have expressed their determination to bring about a merger of these various European Communities.[20]) This Court was constituted to ensure the rule of law in the interpretation and application of community norms by hearing cases of violations, including violations by member states which have been charged by the now merged executive organs of the three Communities (the Commission of the E.E.C., the High Authority of the E.C.S.C., and the Commission of Euratom) with failure to comply with the treaty provisions of the Communities.[21] In at least two cases member states which had been charged with refusal to

[18] Root, "The Sanction Of International Law," in *Addresses On International Subjects by Elihu Root* 30–1 (Bacon and Scott, eds., 1916, reprinted in McDougal and Feliciano at 274).

[19] Anderson, "Questions in Russia," *N. Y. Times*, Aug. 27, 1968, p. 1. Cf. the following editorial on the Czechoslovakia crisis, *N. Y. Times*, Aug. 24, 1968, p. 28:

> Cynics in the Kremlin and elsewhere may ask, as did Stalin with reference to the Pope, "How many divisions does the U. N. have?" But those who would simply write off the long-run impact of world opinion can be as wrong as those who expect too much from the United Nations.

[20] Treaty Establishing A Single Council And A Single Commission of the European Communities, preamble, unofficial transl. in Stein and Hay, *Documents For Law and Institutions in the Atlantic Area* 194 (1967).

[21] See European Economic Community Treaty, signed March 25, 1957, 298 U.N.T.S. 11, Art. 169:

> If the Commission considers that a Member State has failed to fulfill any of its obligations under the Treaty, it shall give a reasoned opinion on the matter after requiring such state to submit its comments.
>
> If such State does not comply with the terms of such opinion within the period laid down by the Commission, the latter may refer the matter to the Court of Justice.

The European Atomic Energy Community Treaty, signed March 25, 1957, 298 U.N.T.S.

comply with official directives, are reported to have been moved to compliance after referral of their cases to the Court, and thus to the possibility of receiving an adverse judgment.[22] The distinguished President of the Court, Judge A. M. Donner, has attested to the effectiveness of the power of public condemnation, as compared with economic measures, in these words:

> Experience shows that the pressure of public opinion is a much more effective sanction and States – at least European States – must be supposed to submit to judicial rulings. More important is the fact that member states may be summoned before the Court of the High Authority and the Commissions to hear their action or inaction condemned in law.[23]

May not the lesson of this European experience be transposed to the larger global arena? Is it not possible that the pressure of world public opinion may be marshaled through the establishment of a procedure designed for the public censure of any government found inflicting unauthorized violence upon the international community?

Certainly no inherent equation bars the community from devising a medium for the objective scrutiny of its most pressing problem.

The Choice of Medium

The medium could be an existing organ such as the General Assembly.[24] Or it could be a new institution, custom-made for the purpose.

167, Art. 141 is comparable. See further European Coal and Steel Community Treaty, signed April 18, 1950, 261 U.N.T.S. 140, Art. 88:

> If the High Authority considers that a State has failed in one of the obligations incumbent upon it by virtue of this Treaty, it shall, after permitting the State in question to present its views, take note of the failure in a reasoned decision accompanied by a justification. It shall allow the State in question a period of time within which to provide for the execution of its obligations.
>
> Such a State may appeal to the Court's general jurisdiction within a period of two months from the notification of the decision.

[22] See European Economic Community, *Seventh General Report* 335 (1964); and European Coal and Steel Community, *Ninth General Report* 173 (1961). See also discussion of the case of DeBecker v. Belgium, referred by the European Commission of Human Rights (1960) to the European Court of Human Rights with effect on a government's legislative action before judgment, in Robertson, *Human Rights In Europe* 63–8 (1963).

[23] Donner, "The Court of Justice of the European Communities," *International and Comparative Law Quarterly, Supp. No. 1*, 66, 71 (1961).

[24] See, e.g., the use of General Assembly Resolution 2324 (XXII), which:

> Condemns the illegal arrest, deportation and trial at Pretoria of the thirty-seven South West Africans as a flagrant violation by the Government of South Africa of their rights, of the international status of the Territory and of General Assembly Resolution 2145 (XXI). ...

The General Assembly

The most appropriate forum for the arbitrament of state-sponsored transnational violence is probably not the General Assembly – by reason of its voting procedure. Like the voting procedure of the Security Council, which is warped by a veto-implemented cold war partisanship, the voting procedure of the General Assembly, though free of veto, is not free of partisanship.

At first it might seem proper that an accused state be made to answer for its anti-social behavior before an assembly of other states. Like the accused individual whose cause is decided by a jury in some legal systems, it is arguable that an accused state ought to be judged by its peers. However, to say that a governmental body called before the General Assembly for judgment would be judged by its peers, means in fact that it would be judged by its allies and competitors. Unlike an accused individual before a jurybox filled with strangers, a state accused before the General Assembly would find itself standing before a panel of sovereign jurors subject to no challenge for any cause relating to partisanship, conflict of interest or other bias. Under such conditions of prejudicial risk a vote of condemnation or acquittal in the General Assembly, no matter how fair and objective in itself, would be overshadowed by the problem of its credibility in the eyes of the community as an impartial decision. It would be too easy for a censured state to protest that the decision was political rather than legal.

The moral efficacy of any judgment of condemnation would be compromised in the eyes of the community so long as the impartiality of its method of production could not be certified. The General Assembly's voting procedure, however satisfactory it may be for other purposes, does not provide this certification. Even the best procedure, when compromised with prejudice, becomes a moral cripple and alienates the confidence which underlies public opinion.

An International Peace Court

Our reservations as to the fitness of the decisional apparatus of the Security Council and the General Assembly for the public assessment of international violence suggest by contrast the specifications of an organ that can merit public confidence in the performance of this delicate and critical function. They suggest the desirability of a forum of judgment which features visible safeguards against obvious partisanship, which excludes the veto, and which specializes in impartiality.

These are the specifications of a judicial tribunal. Function suggests that it be called the International Peace Court.

V

THE COURT IN DESIGN

Qualified by centuries of specialization in impartial decision, the judicial tribunal emerges as the most appropriate medium for utilizing the instrument of modern communication in a strategy of public judgment directed to the deterrence of state-sponsored violence. The court brings impartiality to judgment.

And the courtroom brings formality. The formal manner provides a natural setting for the serious matter. It tends to promote the commitment to objectivity which it symbolizes.

Impartiality and commitment tend to inspire confidence.

Public confidence in the judicial function is particularly served, however, by openness. Judgment behind closed doors impairs public accountability. The open court, by contrast, is seen to be one that is willing to take the risk of public scrutiny. It is not enough that justice be done; it must be seen to be done.

If it would merit the confidence of the community, however, the open, formal, impartial tribunal must be structured for effectiveness and legitimacy as well as for a wide base of supporting participation.

In the following pages, the possible structural variants for an International Peace Court will be weighed in the scales of effectiveness. The resulting selection will then be assessed for legitimacy and for participational capacity.

Effective Structure

The selection of the most effective judicial structure for an International Peace Court may be made from four basic structural alternatives: (a) a national court, (b) the International Court of Justice, (c) an *ad hoc* special tribunal and (d) a permanent special tribunal.

A National Court

(a) One possibility would be to use the resources of an available national court. The manifest advantage of a national court is economy. The use of presently available national judicial systems would obviate the expense, albeit limited, of constituting and maintaining a new international tribunal.

The probable disadvantage of a national court, however, would consist in a low visibility of impartiality depending on the nature of the relationship known or thought to exist between the court's host state and the adjudged state.[1] A nationally supported court would ordinarily not be expected to compete with an international tribunal in making visible that impartiality in international decision-making which would be indispensable to the public acceptance of its decisions.

In balancing the scales between economy and impartiality, therefore, the factor of impartiality would clearly seem to outweigh the opposed factor of limited cost.

The International Court Of Justice

(b) It would be possible to make an International Peace Court out of a chamber of the International Court of Justice. The Statute of the International Court of Justice empowers that Court to form chambers of three or more judges devoted to particular categories of cases.[2] One such chamber might be devoted to the category of transnational violence.

The advantage of the International Court of Justice is that it combines the economy of present availability with the attribute of generally recognized impartiality.

The disadvantage is that it suffers from a constitutionally limited capacity for jurisdiction as to parties, a jurisdictional capacity which falls short of the competency to consider the conduct of any state which does not consent to be judged.[3] The unlikelihood of such consent on

[1] Cf. the observation with reference to cold war partisanship in Sohn, "Adjudication and Enforcement in Arms Control," in Brennan (ed.), *Arms Control, Disarmament and National Security* 368 (1961):

> Unfortunately, there is little inclination on either side to trust the judicial system of the other, and only a true international solution would be acceptable to all concerned.

[2] Statute of the International Court of Justice (hereinafter cited Stat. I. C. J.), Art. 26(1):

> The Court may from time to time form one or more chambers, composed of three or more judges as the Court may determine, for dealing with particular categories of cases; for example, labor cases and cases relating to transit and communications.

[3] Stat. I. C. J., Art. 34 (1):

> Only states may be parties in cases before the Court.

Art. 36 (1):

the part of any offending state provides, unfortunately, a crippling stricture on the Court's serviceability for the deterrence of violence through the judgment of state conduct.

A Special Tribunal

(c) The serious drawbacks associated with existing national courts and the International Court of Justice point to the feasibility of establishing a special tribunal designed without disabilities relating to impartiality and jurisdictional competence. The need, accordingly, is for a tribunal which is specially designed to judge the offender without his consent. The deterrent promise of such a jurisdictional breakthrough would seem sufficient warrant for whatever may be the cost of creating a special tribunal which can provide it.

The remaining question is whether the special tribunal's status should be *ad hoc* or permanent. The former would be constituted anew as each case arises. An *ad hoc* tribunal would have the advantage of being more economical, if the occasions for resort to its services were so infrequent as to preclude the need for continuing maintenance.

A Permanent Special Tribunal

(d) With the prevailing high frequency of transnational violence, it would probably prove more economical to maintain a standing judicial structure than to reconstitute a series of structures on demand in the individual cases. A permanent tribunal would probably be more conducive to the development of a consistent body of case law than would a series of temporary tribunals.[4] It would be more conducive to the development of the expertise and therefore of the efficiency of the men who operate it.[5] Finally, the abiding presence of a peace tribunal among the nations would constitute a symbol of deterrence and a standing reminder of the international community's readiness for judgment.

The jurisdiction of the Court comprises all cases which the parties refer to it and all matters specially provided for in the Charter of the United Nations or in treaties and conventions in force.

[4] See Fachiri, *The Permanent Court of International Justice* 104 (1932):

. . . it is one of the Court's most important and valuable functions to build up a coherent international jurisprudence by means of its decisions. Moreover, it is part of the inherent nature of judicial bodies to follow their own decisions in subsequent cases to which they are applicable.

[5] Cf. Jackson, "Organizing for Survival," 38 *Foreign Affairs* 446, 447 (1960):

The plain fact is that good policy demands both good men and good machinery. And though it may be true that good men can triumph over poor machinery, it is also true that they are more effective when they work with good machinery.

This weighing of the given alternative structures in the functional scales of value thus settles on the permanent special international tribunal as the most appropriate institutional format for the public judgment of violence in the world.

Legitimacy

The projection of an International Peace Court for the effective application of global norms in regulation of transnational violence rests on a rationale of deterrence mediated through the influence of the Court's judgment upon community judgment and the consequent impact of community judgment upon the minds of potential violators. The effective influence of the Court accordingly will be a factor of its legitimacy or authoritative status, that is, of its compatibility with the values and expectations of the community.

It would be possible to set up a court without community support. Such a court could go through the motions of calling witnesses, holding hearings and convicting a party of guilt for violation of law. But its judgment would carry no authority.[6]

The most comprehensive articulation of the expectations of the international community relating to the maintenance of peace and security is the Charter of the United Nations. On the 26th of June, 1945, in the city of San Francisco,[7] these expectations converged to utter a preamble to the Charter:

> We The Peoples Of The United Nations Determined to save succeeding generations from the scourge of war, which twice in our lifetime has brought untold sorrow to mankind, and...
>
> to unite our strength to maintain international peace and security, and
>
> to ensure, by the acceptance of principles and the institution of methods, that armed force shall not be used, save in the common interest...
>
> Have Resolved To Combine Our Efforts To Accomplish These Aims
>
> Accordingly, our respective Governments, through representatives assembled in the city of San Francisco who have exhibited their full powers found to be in good and due form, have agreed to the present Charter of the United Nations and do hereby establish an international organization to be known as the United Nations.

[6] Compare, e.g., the War Crimes Tribunal sponsored by Bertrand Russell and convened in London, November 13, 1966. See Russell, *War Crimes in Vietnam* 125–30 (1967). Sitting in Stockholm, Sweden and Roskilde, Denmark, the Tribunal convicted the United States of various war crimes in May and Dec., 1967. See *N. Y. Times* Dec. 2, 1967, p. 3.

[7] U. N. Charter, Art. 111.

As of November 12, 1968 one hundred twenty-six nations of the world have endorsed this formulation of community expectation[8] by subscribing to the United Nations Charter.

Tacit Authorization Of The United Nations Charter

The first evidence of the compatibility of the projected International Peace Court with the world community's authority system is by way of negative clearance: the Charter contains no prohibition of special tribunals. From this absence of prohibition in what purports to be a comprehensive normative document, we can infer a tacit permissibility, on the premise distilled by Hans Kelsen that – "the legal order permits the behavior of an individual when the legal order does not obligate the individual to behave otherwise."[9] The Charter's non-prohibition is a tacit authorization.

Such a broad permissibility abstracted from the absence of prohibition in the United Nations Charter would seem sufficient, if not strikingly visible, authorization for the establishment of an International Peace Court.

General Authorization of Article 95

Supplemental authority, however, might add persuasive weight, particularly if it were made visible, in the words of Edmond Cahn – "not with loose abstractions but with specific texts...."[10]

The task of winning acceptance for any new enterprise is likely to be facilitated if appeal can be made for reliance upon express supporting propositions which themselves enjoy wide acceptance. In this instance, further authority may, indeed, be adduced from the visible text of the Charter.

Express permission for the establishment of tribunals for the solution of international differences is set forth as an incident of the Charter's authorization for the establishment of the principal judicial organ of the United Nations, the International Court of Justice. This is found in Article 95:

> Nothing in the present Charter shall prevent Members of the United Nations from entrusting the solution of their differences to other tribunals by virtue of agreements already in existence or which may be concluded in the future.

[8] See *N. Y. Times*, November 13, 1968, p. 3:
United Nations, N. Y., Nov. 12 –
Equatorial Guinea, a former Spanish colony on the west coast of Africa, became the 126th member of the United Nations today.

[9] Kelsen, *Pure Theory of Law* 246 (2d rev'd ed., transl. Knight, 1967).

[10] Cahn, *The Predicament of Democratic Man* 33 (1961).

This passage anchors the authoritative status of the projected special tribunal in the visible support of express language. The intendment is that other tribunals are not incompatible with the World Court. The case in defense of the legitimacy of the Court could well rest at this point.

Specific Authorization Of Article 52

It may be possible, nevertheless, to corroborate the broad wording of Article 95 with more specific contextual reference. Article 52, paragraph 1, seems to do just this. Whereas Article 95 tells us, in effect, that tribunals for solving differences among states are a legitimate subject for international organization relating to the settlement of differences between states, Article 52 (1) says that international organizations for dealing with matters of international peace may have a regional basis:

Nothing in the present Charter precludes the existence of regional arrangements or agencies for dealing with such matters relating to the maintenance of international peace and security as are appropriate for regional action, provided that such arrangements or agencies and their activities are consistent with the Purposes and Principles of the United Nations.

It is submitted that the subject matter of Article 95 may be subsumed under the authorization contained in the language of Article 52 (1) in that a "tribunal" is simply a particular form of "agency," and that if it is organized by any number of nations less than the full membership of the United Nations, it would qualify as "regional." (The meaning of "regional" is probed below in the next section). Together the two provisions provide a framework of authority for an international tribunal organized on a regional base.

This supportive framework is useful in providing a rational nexus between such a tribunal and the general structure of global authority.[11] Just as Article 95 guarantees the compatibility of the existence of the tribunal as an agency for the arbitrament of international differences with the existence of the International Court of Justice, as the "principal judicial organ of the United Nations," so Article 52 (1) guarantees

[11] The importance of this function in the U. N. Charter provision, in contrast to its absence in the Covenant of the League of Nations, was noted in Bebr, "Regional Organizations: A United Nations Problem," 49 *American Journal of International Law* 162, 168 (1955):

> Because of a complete lack of any provision in the Covenant formalizing the relation of regional organizations to the world institution, none of the regional organizations of that period stood in a clearly defined relation to the League. The Charter of the United Nations represents an advance in this respect. The Charter provisions disclose an attempt to relate the regional organizations to the world organization and to reconcile the principles of universalism and regionalism.

the compatibility of the tribunal as a regional agency with the United Nations, in the requirement that the agency be consistent with the purposes and principles of the United Nations. Even more specifically, Article 52 (1) implies the compatibility of such a regional agency with the primary responsibility of the Security Council in that the article countenances a limited responsibility in the regional agency for "dealing with such matters relating to the maintenance of international peace and security as are appropriate for regional action...." It may be submitted that the disappointing and unpromising record of an ideologically divided Security Council in controlling international violence supplies this required appropriateness for regional action.

The Charter's authorization of regional agency responsibility for peace and security contains an operational restraint. Article 53(1) provides that – "no enforcement action shall be taken under regional arrangements or by regional agencies without the authorization of the Security Council...." This restraint would not impair the tribunal's activities, which will consist in the exercise of judgment, not of enforcement. Hence the tribunal will enjoy the bonus of compatibility with the activity of the Security Council without the onus of dependence upon its veto.

The use of Article 52 (1) with its endorsement of regional agencies would thus provide a kind of symbolic connective tissue between the tribunal as a limited authority structure and the United Nations as a global structure of authority. It would also highlight the tribunal's synchronization with the general trend of nations toward formation of regional groupings, such as those of the European Communities.[12]

And so the legal footing of the proposed tribunal can be grounded on the most authoritative articulation of the international community's expectations – the United Nations Charter. The Charter tacitly authorizes special tribunals by not forbidding them. The Charter expressly authorizes special tribunals in Article 95. If further corroboration is sought, it may be reasonably argued that Article 52 (1), authorizing regional agencies for dealing with matters of peace and security, would be applicable to a peace tribunal viewed as a regional agency. The propriety of so viewing the projected tribunal is elaborated in the next section.

These several strands of authorization threading through the fabric

[12] Cf. Haas, "The Challenge of Regionalism," XII *International Organization* 441 (1958): The most interesting challenge inherent in the study of regionalism lies in the potentialities of the field for insights into the process of community formation at the international level.

of the articulated expectations of the community intertwine to form a cordon of support for an international tribunal projected for organization on a less than universal base of participation, and for investiture with competence to deal with those matters relating to the maintenance of international peace and security which can be reached through the adjudication of violence. It seems reasonable to conclude, therefore, that the authoritative status of an International Peace Court is secure in the official texts which reflect community understanding.

The texts, however, are but a minimal statement of authority. The fullness of the tribunal's authority will ultimately be measured in the respect which it commands in the community of nations. The earnest of their respect will be their participation in the enterprise. The wider the participation, the greater the respect. The greater the respect, the greater will be the tribunal's influence for peace. The words of Chief S. O. Adebo of Nigeria, uttered in reference to the International Court of Justice, may be applied to an International Peace Court:

> ...at the national or international level, the Court will in the last resort secure only the degree of acceptance that it has earned and deserves.[13]

Participants

For most effective influence, the organization of an International Peace Court, as proposed, will require the participation of many nations. No legal restriction on participation would follow from the wide latitude of authoritative support for the Court construed in the Charter's tacit permission as well as in the express permission of Article 95 of the Charter. The question may arise, however, whether extensive participation would be compatible with the corroborative base of authoritative support which has been argued from the Charter's authorization of a regional activity in Article 52 (1).

Although the conventional meaning of the term "regional" would appear to be restrictive by implication of geographic proximity, the history of the Charter text supports a non-restrictive construction. When the question of definition was presented to the cognizant sub-

[13] Center for the Study of Democratic Institutions, "Report on Pacem In Terris II," 1 *The Center Magazine* 59 (Oct.–Nov. 1967). Cf., e.g., the observation of Gormley, "Individual Petition To The Commission Of The European Economic Community," 1 *Valparaiso Univ. Law Review* 255, 281 (1967):

> ... the mass outcry in Africa, Asia, Latin America, and Europe against the Hague Court's refusal to examine the merits [case of South West Africa, Second Phase Judgment, I.C.J. Reports 1966, p. 6], indicates the popular reaction that can arise from a major judicial default.

division (The Subcommittee of Committee 4 of Commission III) of the United Nations Conference On International Organization, the drafting organ of the United Nations' Charter, a restrictive meaning was proffered and rejected. The occasion of this rejection was the submission by the Egyptian Delegation of a draft which would have inserted a definition in the text of the then proposed Charter, as follows:

There shall be considered as regional arrangements organizations of a permanent nature grouping in a given geographical area several countries which, by reason of their proximity, community of interests or cultural, linguistic, historical or spiritual affinities, make themselves jointly responsible for the peaceful settlement of any disputes which may arise between them and for the maintenance of peace and security in their region, as well as for the safeguarding of their interests and the development of their economic and cultural relations.[14]

The Subcommittee rejected this restrictive draft definition of "regional arrangement" preferring to leave the meaning open-ended in the interest of comprehensiveness, and reported that:

Against the argument of the Delegate of Egypt it was contended that definition was undesirable within a General Charter such as was in course of preparation; that definition would precipitate lengthy debate; and that it was legitimate to doubt whether the definition would prove sufficiently comprehensive.[15]

A comprehensive construction of "regional" finds support in the scholarly concurrence of the eminent commentators of the United Nations Charter, Goodrich and Hambro. This is their comment on the Egyptian Construction:

This amendment was considered by a subcommittee of Committee III/4 and by the Committee itself and was rejected on the ground that while it "clearly defined obvious legitimate and eligible factors for a regional arrangement" it probably failed to cover all the situations which might be covered by regional arrangements. The phrase "regional arrangements" as used in this and other articles of the Charter obviously does have a wider scope than the Egyptian amendment would admit. In Article 53... it is made to apply to mutual assistance treaties entered into between states which are wholly lacking in geographical propinquity or in the other common interests enumerated in the Egyptian proposal.[16]

An example of the last reference would seem to be the North Atlantic Treaty, which Kelsen identifies as a regional arrangement.[17] Goodrich and Hambro include in "regional arrangements and agencies" the Commonwealth of Nations.[18]

[14] Doc. WD 70, III/4/A/11, June 2, 1945, 12 *United Nations Conference on International Organization* 857–58 (1945).

[15] *Ibid.*

[16] Goodrich and Hambro, *Charter of the United Nations* 311 (2d rev. ed., 1949).

[17] Kelsen, *The Law of the United Nations* 320, note 4 (1950). NATO membership includes the United States and European states. See North Atlantic Treaty, *U. S. Treaties and Other International Acts Series* 1964; 34 U.N.T.S. 243.

[18] *Supra* note 16 at 311–12.

The comprehensive construction does not go so far as to deprive "regional" of all import of restriction. Kelson's construction reconciles comprehensiveness with some connotation of geographic limitation by interpreting the term "regional arrangements" to mean "treaties concluded by some, not by all, Members of the United Nations," while noting that "the wording of paragraph 1 does not exclude treaties concluded by Members with non-members."[19]

A liberal construction such as Kelsen's would seem to "prove sufficiently comprehensive," in keeping with the standard of the Charter's framers. It allows for any level of international organization between the national and the global levels. A restrictive construction on the other hand would limit the use of Article 52 (1) to closely grouped nations, thereby omitting a middle level of potential organization located above the level of the small neighborhood of states and below the level of the total international community or of the official structure of the United Nations. (One might prefer for convenience to refer to the middle level as "superregional.") Such an omission would seem to be functionally arbitrary as well as inconsistent with the framer's comprehensive perspective. The Charter places no limitation of size on the meaning of "regional." It does not preclude a big regional organization. A regional agency may be an international grouping of any size below the global level.

Therefore, viewed as an application of Article 95, an International Peace Court would be under no constitutional restriction of participation in its original and sustaining organization. All interested states would be eligible as participants. Even treating the International Peace Court as a regional agency under Article 52 (1) and viewing such a regional agency as one having a less than global base of organizational support, no nation would be denied opportunity by reason of geographic location to participate in the organization of the Court. Eligibility to

[19] *Supra* note 17 at 319–20, reading in part:

> As used in Chapter VIII of the Charter which bears the heading: "Regional Arrangements" (without reference to regional "agencies"), the term "regional" has also the connotation of "partial," that is to say, treaties concluded only by a part of the Members of the United Nations, and, hence, constituting only partial communities as compared with the total community: The United Nations. It stands to reason that such treaties are concluded to satisfy certain common interests of the contracting parties. The community of interests may – but need not necessarily be – based on their geographical propinquity. There is good reason to assume that, according to the intention of the framers of the Charter, the meaning of the term "regional arrangements" is wider than that of treaties concluded by neighbouring states.

participate would be based on moral commitment, not on geographic circumstance – on shared objectives, not on shared borders.

Summary

Out of the analysis of this chapter there emerges the design of an International Peace Court having these three features:

1) Structure – the Court has the form of a permanent special tribunal.
2) Legitimacy – the Court not only does not conflict with the pattern of authority concretized in the United Nations Charter, but finds affirmative support therein.
3) Participants – the enterprise of founding and sustaining the court is open to the active support of all those states, including any of the major powers, which suscribe to its purpose and action.

VI

THE COURT IN ACTION

An International Peace Court will be structured for action. Our attention now moves from the requirements of the structure to the componentry of the action and the requirements for its effective impact.

The product of the action will be the judgment. The judgment will be produced in the process of applying the law to a determinate set of facts. The facts will be determined from the evidence. The evidence will be presented by the parties and tried to the Court. The whole operation will be activated by claims interposed by a party complainant and a party defendant. The party complainant, or plaintiff, will be a state or states alleging the perpetration of impermissible violence by another state. The defendant will be the other state. The complainant will submit its claim to the judges, that they may try the facts, apply the law and enter the judgment. This they will do by virtue of, and within the bounds of, the jurisdiction or authorized adjudicatory power entrusted to them by the organizers of the Court acting within the larger framework of global community authority.

Thus outlined in teleological order, the components of the action of the Court will include the judgment, the applying of law, the trying of facts, claims, parties, judges, and jurisdiction. Reversing the order according to temporal sequence these components will now be considered in turn, starting with jurisdiction.

Jurisdiction

An international Peace Court will be authorized for a specific purpose: the public judgment of state-sponsored violence. Hence the scope of its jurisdiction will be special rather than general, being limited to the subject matter of transnational violence. Jurisdiction limited as to subject matter, however, need not be limited as to territory. There are two realistic options relating to the range of the Court's territorial purview. It may cover only cases occurring within the aggregate of the territories of those states participating in the organization of the Court, or it may be universal.

In support of the former option one might argue that an innovating court in international relations should be jurisdictionally conservative. Not to be obvious in the practice of self-restraint, arguably, would be to compromise public acceptance of its decisions. Not to adhere strictly to established legal convention would conceivably risk offending general expectations. The limited territorial basis of jurisdiction would seem to be the most firmly rooted in legal convention.

In support of the option of universal territorial jurisdiction, however, it may be pointed out that there is precedent in the practice of national tribunals for the assertion of jurisdiction over acts occurring outside the territory of the forum. The international community recognises a latitude of jurisdictional principles. Thus many states assert jurisdiction as to territorially external offences with internal effects, and many recognize a principle of universality in asserting jurisdiction as to piracy on the high seas having no physical contact with the territory of the forum, but causing nearly universal concern to the international community.[1] It would not tax the imagination of man to bring acts of transnational violence within these recognised jurisdictional tolerances. Violence against any member of the world neighborhood is a matter of concern to all its neighbors. If the universal repercussions of such behavior are not physical, they at least are psychological. The repercussions of a nuclear explosion, indeed, can be borne physically as well as psychologically to the remotest shores, affecting the national interests of many states indiscriminately.

In the context of expanding international violence, it can hardly be insisted in seriousness that the assertion of universal territorial jurisdiction by an International Peace Court will affront community expectations sustaining the existing legal order. This consideration is underlined by the absence of any proposal to execute the Court's authority by resort to a military or an economic sanction. In the projected International Peace Court the sole sanction is the judgment itself. Warrant emerges for the conclusion, therefore, that the Court's exercise of jurisdiction over acts of transnational violence without terri-

[1] See Bishop, *International Law* 463–64, note (2d ed. 1962). See also Briggs, *The Law Of Nations* 575–76 (1952), quoting the Harvard Research In International Law, "Draft Convention On Jurisdiction With Respect To Crime" (1935).

torial restriction would not really offend community expectations. On the contrary, a rule which would constrict the jurisdiction of the Court by reason of territory might risk disappointing the very expectations raised by the Court itself – expectations raised by the appearance on the international scene of a forum professedly devoted to the public judgment of acts which by their virulent nature are themselves no respecter of territory in their threat to the whole community. It is the provision of immunity from judgment by circumstance of geography which would appear to be without warrant.

A responsible definition of the jurisdictional role of an International Peace Court, therefore, would seem to require that the Court never refuse to receive a case of transnational violence by reason of its place of origin.

Judges

The respect accorded the Court by the international community will be a factor not only of the scope of its jurisdictional role but of the status of its personnel. Hence the need for constitutional standards relating to the selection and qualification of judges. Fortunately, the task at hand need not proceed from pure speculation. It can draw upon the experience of the international community. Out of this experience have come outstanding models of judicial standards, in particular, those of two highly respected international tribunals: The International Court of Justice and the Court of Justice of The European Communities. The constitutional provisions of both tribunals are prototypes of workable procedures to assure judicial impartiality and competence.

Impartiality

An obvious threat to judicial impartiality on an international bench in a world of competing nations would be any influence emanating from the individual judges' national backgrounds. Both the International Court of Justice and the European Court of Justice provide safeguards to insulate their judges from such influence. These safeguards seek to secure judicial independence at three critical points of possible judicial vulnerability to national control, namely, appointment, remuneration, and removal.

The prerogative of judicial appointment in the case of both tribunals is lodged in supporting institutions of international composition – not in the judges' respective governments of origin. In the case of the International Court of Justice election is by absolute majority vote of the General Assembly and the Security Council from a list of persons nominated by the national groups in the Permanent Court of Arbitration.[2]

In the case of the European Court of Justice, judges are chosen by the governments comprising the membership of the European Communities acting in common agreement.[3]

Remunerational independence is secured for the International Court of Justice by constitutive provisions requiring salaries, allowances, compensation and pensions to be fixed by the General Assembly, as well as requiring the salaries, allowances and compensation to be free of all taxation, and requiring Court expenses to be borne by the United Nations as decided by the General Assembly.[4]

The budget of the European Court of Justice has been made the responsibility of the European Communities.[5]

The power to dismiss a judge from either tribunal is placed outside the reach of national control and reserved to the unanimous decision of his benchmates.[6]

Competence

Constitutive provisions of both tribunals require that judges be selected from persons of acknowledged juristic competence.

In the case of the European Court appointments shall be from among persons of recognized independence and ability.[7]

In the case of the International Court of Justice it is provided that:

> The Court shall be composed of a body of independent judges, elected regardless of their nationality from among persons of high moral character, who possess the qualifications required in their respective countries for appointment to the highest judicial offices, or are jurisconsults of recognized competence in international law.[8]

The Lesson Of The Central American Court Of Justice

The standards of judicial selection and qualification which have ripened in the International Court of Justice and the European Court

[2] Stat. I.C.J., Arts. 4, 10.

[3] European Economic Community Treaty (hereinafter cited E.E.C. Treaty), Art. 167.

[4] Stat. I.C.J., Arts. 32, 33.

[5] See European Coal and Steel Community Treaty (hereinafter cited E.C.S.C. Treaty), Art. 78, and European Economic Community Treaty (hereinafter cited E.E.C. Treaty) Arts. 199–209.

[6] Stat. I.C.J., Art. 18; Protocol On The Statute Of The Court Of Justice Of The E.E.C. (annexed to E.E.C. Treaty, hereinafter cited Protocol), Art. 6.

[7] See E.E.C. Treaty, Art. 167.

[8] Stat. I.C.J., Art. 2.

of Justice may be to some extent the fruitage of the experience of the late Central American Court of Justice.[9] This tribunal functioned from 1908 to 1918 as an international organ for the resolution of disputes between El Salvador, Nicaragua, Costa Rica, Honduras, and Guatemala.[10] The fact that its judges were beholden to their respective governments of origin for their appointment and apparently for their remuneration helps to explain the early demise of the Central American Court of Justice. This is the view of Manley Hudson, who concluded that:

> Unfortunately, the Justices of the court seem never to have been looked upon as international officials of all five states; instead, they were usually regarded as officials of their respective states.[11]

The experience of the Central American Court of Justice served to expose the flaws that had to be removed from the evolving international judicature.[12] That court was followed by the Permanent Court of International Justice and the European Court of Justice in the line of advancing international judicial experience. The legacy of this cumulative experience is a body of canons of impartiality and competence to guide the next stage in international judicial evolution.

National And Cultural Balance

If judicial evolution is to be advanced through the development of an International Peace Court, it is important not only that the judges of such a Court be qualified individually, but that the Court as a body observe standards of impartiality and competence that will make it credible to all parts of the community.[13]

Corporate impartiality will be promoted by national and cultural balance in the membership of the bench. Both the International Court

[9] See generally Hudson, "The Central American Court of Justice," 26 *American Journal of International Law* 759 (1932).

[10] See *ibid.*

[11] *Id.*, p. 763.

[12] See *Working Paper, World Peace Through the Rule of Law, First World Conference, June 30–July 6, 1963, Athens, Greece*, page 77:

> The Central American Court in any event served as a useful precedent to succeeding international tribunals ....
>
> Thus, for example, greater steps were taken towards assuring the independence of judges appointed to the later Permanent Court of International Justice because many felt that one of the weaknesses of the Central American Court was the fact that each judge served essentially as a representative of his country since he was both elected and paid by his government.

[13] Cf. the admonition of Arthur Larson in *When Nations Disagree* 5 (1961):

> that many of the people of the world do not regard present international law and tribunals as their law and their tribunals.

Of Justice and the European Court of Justice have built-in safeguards for averting imbalance.

The Statute of the International Court of Justice prescribes that judges shall be elected regardless of nationality,[14] that no two of them may be nationals of the same state,[15] and that in any proceeding a state litigant before the court shall be able to choose a judge if none from among its own nationals already sits on the court.[16] National balance is assured in the case of the European Court through the aforementioned requirement of appointment by agreement among the governments of the member states.

Cultural balance will be promoted by representation of the various legal systems and cultures upon the bench. The relevance of catholicity of representation to the corporate impartiality and competence of the bench is reflected in this exemplary provision for the International Court of Justice:

> At every election, the electors shall bear in mind not only that the persons to be elected should individually possess the qualifications required, but also that in the body as a whole the representation of the main forms of civilization and of the principal legal systems of the world should be assured.[17]

Parties

Acceptance by the international community of the judgment of an International Peace Court finding a government guilty of illegality through violence will depend on the community's recognition of the impartiality of the judgment, a recognition which will be conditioned upon the impartiality not only of the Court's judges but also of the procedure defining in detail the opportunity of the parties to be heard by the Court.

When one nation comes before the Court with the claim that a second nation has perpetrated unauthorized violence and with the request that the Court make a factual finding and legal judgment upon the conduct of the second nation, procedural impartiality requires that an adequate opportunity to be heard be accorded both parties, the complainant nation and the defendant nation. Moreover, any hearing on the legality of transnational violence involves the entire community

[14] Stat. I.C.J., Art. 2.
[15] *Id.*, Art. 3.
[16] *Id.*, Art. 31.
[17] *Id.*, Art. 9.

of nations as a real party in interest. The community is present to oversee the observance of its overarching interest.

Party Complainant

It is axiomatic that the complainant be heard by the Court and have the right of representation by counsel.[18] The complaining party normally would be a state which considers either itself or another state to be the target of violence. A procedural variant might be provided, however, permitting the complaint to be brought by a public prosecutor representing all the states participating in the organization of the Court. This arrangement would be appropriate when the aggrieved state is deterred from filing a complaint by duress or other reason.

Party Defendant

Impartiality requires that the defendant be given equal opportunity to be heard, an opportunity perfected in the right to the assistance of counsel. Implicit in the right to a hearing is the right to adequate notification of the complaint and its allegations as well as provision for adequate time to prepare an answer as well as the right to a bill of particulars in clarification of unclear allegations. In the event of defendant's default in answering the complaint, by reason of its refusal to recognize the Court's jurisdiction or its failure to appear, such default should not be permitted to stand in the way of the Court's consideration of the merits, and rendition of judgment.[19] Nevertheless, in the event of the defendant's failure to appear or to answer the complaint on the merits, procedural impartiality would seem to require judicial appointment of independent legal counsel to represent the defendant state on the merits before any adverse decision be taken against its interests.

Apart from its function in promoting impartiality and fair play for the parties, the appointment of counsel to represent the non-cooperating defendant state may have the spin-off effect of putting pressure on the defendant state to cooperate. Thus, conceivably, the situation might arise where appointed counsel's brief for the defense could be strengthened by making available to him evidence in the possession of the absentee defendant state. Rather than stand by while its unaided court-appointed counsel attempts to make a defense, under such a handicap, to its own detriment, the state in question might decide that

[18] See Protocol, Art. 17.
[19] Cf. Stat. I.C.J., Art. 53; Protocol, Art. 38.

the better part of prudence would be to cooperate in defending the charge against it. A domestic analogy would be the situation where a party being sued receives the assistance of the party ultimately liable on the issue brought by the plaintiff. There is a perceivable advantage in assisting the person who asserts one's own freedom from liability. The appointment of defense counsel may thus serve to elicit the defendant's cooperation.

Impartiality would be further enhanced by providing the defendant with the right of appeal from an adverse decision of the Court. The provision of appeal need not entail creation of a special reviewing tribunal. The International Court of Justice would seem to have the requisite competence for such appellate service,[20] by virtue of its comprehensive jurisdiction as to subject matter in all cases between state parties "which the parties refer to it. . . ."[21] If, however, appellate referral to the World Court is for any reason considered not feasible, or would meet with resistance by litigants, then either an appellate division could be attached to the Peace Court itself, or the services of an outside forum could be obtained for the purpose.

If it should be determined to repose the power of review in some forum other than the Peace Court, such appellate jurisdiction could become a problem if the state complainant before the International Peace Court were to decline to submit to the jurisdiction of the appellate tribunal. This eventuality might be forestalled by requiring, at defendant's option, the complainant's advance submission to appellate jurisdiction at the time it files its complaint in the Peace Court. In practice, however, a complainant with a *bona fide* grievance relating to international violence would seem to have nothing to lose in submitting to a review limited to this issue.

The Presence Of The Community

It is essential not only that justice be done but that it be seen to be done. When adjudication is conducted in the open it is in effect overseen by the general community. Because secrecy has at times been used as a defense mechanism associated with partiality, due process is enhanced in the requirement of open hearings of argument before the International Peace Court. The requirement of openness applied to the

[20] Cf. Hudson, V *International Legislation* 442 (1936), instancing agreement by Czechoslovakia, Jugoslavia, Rumania and Hungary to recognize a right of appeal from judgments of Mixed Arbitral Tribunals to the Permanent Court of International Justice, signed at Paris, April 28, 1930, 121 *League of Nations Treaty Series* 80.

[21] Stat. I.C.J., Art. 36(1).

Court's decisional process would extend to the publication of all proceedings including judgments and their supporting reasons so that the community may appraise the decisions, not on their consonance with popular emotion, but on their rationality. The policy of rationality openly conducted would be further promoted by allowing judges to write independent opinions whether of dissent or of concurrence with the Court's decisions. Professor Paul A. Freund, the distinguished constitutional lawyer, has elaborated the relevance of dissent to public rationality from the practice of dissent in the United States Supreme Court:

> The practice of dissents is a tribute to the force of reason over fiat, and as such it cannot be tolerated where debate would weaken authority....
>
> ...And the Court is like an umpire in that the judges cannot, they must not, measure their success by popular acclaim. But unlike an umpire the Court exposes the reasons for its decisions and even the disagreements entering into them. This practice of candor, which is far from characteristic of courts around the world, presupposes a mature people who in the end will judge their judges rationally.[22]

The priority of community interest will be sustained by making the Court accessible to all states having claims of subjection to violence, even those states not participating in the organization of the Court. It will be sustained particularly in any case of attempted interference with the claim process, through the use of the aforementioned provision for initiation of a claim by a substitute complainant, serving as surrogate either of the aggrieved state or of the community. Whether representing itself or another state, any bona fide complainant before the Court will be the spokesman not just for its exclusive interest but for the inclusive interest of the community of states. The plea of the complainant will strike a blow for the cause of international justice.

The policy of receiving all claims, including those brought against states which either refuse to answer or which reject the Court's jurisdiction, will serve to notify all potential violators that the judgment of the community is not subject to their good pleasure. If unauthorized violence cannot be stopped, it can at least be judged. Judging it may be the first step toward stopping it.

Claims

Claims brought to an International Peace Court will raise two issues: 1) the factual issue, namely, whether an alleged act of international

[22] Freund, *On Law And Justice* 55, 58–59 (1968).

violence was perpetrated by a named state; and 2) the legal issue, namely, whether or not the act if proved, was authorized by community norm.

Included Issues Of A Civil Nature

In some cases the Court may face the necessity of settling an intermediate question of property rights on the way to reaching the issue of breach of the peace. The dilemma of whether one state's troops are in effect domestic police or foreign invaders turns around the issue of title. If title to the land they have occupied is in their own state, the troops are at home on their own soil. If the title, however, is in the other state, then the troops find themselves abroad on foreign soil without authorization.

The unity of the law is demonstrated in this inescapable burden: a tribunal established to determine the legality of violence may find itself obligated to make a determination of a civil nature such as that of land title. The question of where a border runs seems the most likely issue of a civil nature that might require disposition in the course of deciding an issue of violence.

There are alternative responses to the problem of the included civil issue. One policy would be that the Court decline jurisdiction in any case which is not a pure violence case, that is, any case contaminated by an unavoidable civil issue. Against this proposal one visualizes the objection that defendant states wishing to evade jurisdiction would fabricate a convenient civil issue. An alternative policy would be that the Court proceed with all cases and take the included civil matters in stride. However, it might be difficult for the Court to do this without creating the appearance of injustice in a case involving the proprietary or other rights of an absentee defendant state, one that refused to appear in the proceeding.

It does seem unfeasible to set a rigid policy in this area, but the following guidelines may be helpful.

First, the Court may seek to bring the parties to agree to litigate or arbitrate the civil issue separately. If they agree, the Court should suspend its proceedings pending disposition of the civil issue. Once the issue is disposed of, the Court may accept the result and proceed to the ultimate issue. If one party consents to litigate or arbitrate and the other does not, the Court make take note of the fact.

Where the parties do consent to litigate the civil issue, it would perhaps be the better policy for the Court to direct them to another forum of their choice, perhaps the International Court of Justice. The Court would be free to perfect its speciality. Other tribunals are available for the disposition of issues of a civil character. The specialty of an International Peace Court is the adjudication of international violence.

Second, if the parties fail to agree to the separate disposition of the civil issue, the Court may conduct a preliminary inquiry to weigh the community's interest in having the principal issue of violence adjudicated against either or both the parties' interest in not having the secondary issue adjudicated. The principal issue will concern the presence in the community of aggression or breach of peace or threat to peace. The secondary issue will probably concern title to property. In this inquiry the Court may encounter a range of situations along a continuum stretching between two opposite poles. One pole is the case where the issue of violence represents a serious jeopardy to the community and the civil issue represents a slight jeopardy to the parties. The other pole is the case where the issue of violence represents a slight jeopardy to the community and the civil issue represents a serious jeopardy to either party. In this weighing process life should be favored over property.

Third, if the preliminary inquiry issues in the decision to proceed with the principal case, the Court should seek the best evidence available for its resolution of the secondary civil issue. For this it may use the services of appointed experts. In reaching its judgment on the ultimate issue of violence the Court may give some weight to the noted fact of a party's refusal of separate disposition of the civil issue as well as to such a party's participation in any life-endangering acts.

The Court's intervention in the secondary civil issue should only go so far as is necessary to decide the ultimate issue of violence. Consideration of the civil issue would be limited to the purpose of determination of the principal case. This would not signify *res judicata* or collateral estoppel, that is, it would not foreclose reassertion of the civil issue in another case, on another day, in another court.

Fourth, the Court may then give final judgment on the issue of violence. In so doing the Court should indicate to any party objecting to the judgment by reason of the Court's handling of the civil issue, that it stands willing to rehear the case and to vacate the judgment upon the submission of meritorious evidence bearing on the civil issue. The adjudged party is thus given the opportunity for full consideration of its claim, but it has the burden of exercising this opportunity. The community, for its part, is not denied its right to the judgment of violence.

Fifth, if the Court feels that the evidence before it provides an insufficient basis for a rational and just decision, it should have discretion to dismiss the case.

The Issue Of Statehood

One issue that may foreseeably make a frequent appearance before the Court is the issue of statehood – whether a party claiming the prerogatives of a state is or is not a state. The issue is central to the permissible use of force under Article 51 of the United Nations Charter, which reaffirms the "inherent right of individual or collective self-defense if an armed attack occurs against a Member of the United Nations...." Without derogating from the inherent right of states not Members, the passage does refer to the right of states, as only states according to Article 4, can be Members of the United Nations.

The issue can arise in armed conflicts between countrymen who suddenly find themselves separated by a drawn border. The claim to instant statehood by those on one side of the line is implicit in their allegation of the right of self-defense, if they wish to invoke the United Nations Charter. Article 51 of the Charter gives the right of self-defense only to states. The validity of the allegation of statehood becomes essential, therefore, to the legitimacy of any force, individual or collective deployed under this international rubric.

The Charter does not define statehood. While there are generally accepted substantive qualifications for it, consisting of people, territory, government and independent capacity,[23] the Charter lays down no procedure for validating them. Inasmuch as self-validation by any claimant under Article 51 is obviously self-serving, the purpose of the Article would better be served by a more objective certification of an invoker's statehood through third-party review entrusted either to the Security Council[24] or the General Assembly. Provisional certification,

[23] See Briggs, *The Law of Nations* 66 (1952); Bishop, *International Law* 210 (1962).

[24] Cf., e.g., U.N. doc. S/1501, S. C., *Off. Rec., V, 1950*:

The Security Council,

Recalling the finding of the General Assembly in its resolution of 21 October 1949 that the Government of the Republic of Korea is a lawfully established government having effective control and jurisdiction over that part of Korea where the United Nations Temporary Commission on Korea was able to observe and consult and in which the great majority of the people of Korea reside; and that this Government is based on elections which were a valid expression of the free will of the electorate of that part of Korea and which were observed by the Temporary Commission; and that this is the only such Government in Korea; ....

See further Briggs, p. 66:

Nevertheless, determinations of these facts have traditionally been submerged by political considerations.

however, could be supplied in time of crisis by an International Peace Court.

Trying the Facts

The factual issue normally will be litigated upon evidence produced by the parties. The Court will be expected to require the party complainant to make out a *prima facie* case of unauthorized transnational violence against the party defendant before calling upon the defendant to answer the allegation. Beyond these basic expectations, the making of detailed rules of procedure concerning presumption of innocence, burden of proof and other forensic proprieties can be entrusted to the ingenuity and responsibility of the Court. For this purpose the Court can draw upon the experience of the great legal traditions living together in the world community today.

In the trial of facts the Court will have no constitutional power to compel testimony or the production of evidence by an unwilling party defendant. However, the Court can be empowered to take note of the defendant's refusal of testimonial cooperation and conduct its own inquiry into the merits.[25] It may also be empowered to avail itself of the services not only of fact-finding experts but of special advocates attached to the Court to assist it in the determination of questions of both fact and law, somewhat in the manner of the Court advocates appointed in the European Court of Justice for this purpose:

> The function of the Court advocates shall be to present publicly and with complete impartiality and independence oral reasoned arguments on the cases submitted to the Court, in order to assist the Court in the performance of its duties....[26]

Attention has been concentrated upon the desirability of establishing diplomatic relations with the new entity, frequently upon the erroneous assumption that until recognized by a particular State international law did not govern their probably limited relationships. ...
Although the practice of states refutes this assumption ... it seems appropriate today to eliminate the source of confusion – the decentralized determination of the facts – and to provide that the United Nations should establish the criteria of statehood in international law and make provision for collective determinations that a particular entity possesses the required attributes and consequent legal capacity.

[25] Compare the procedure of the World Court in this respect:
"Formal note shall be taken of any refusal," Stat. I.C.J., Art. 49. "The Court may, at any time, entrust any individual, body, bureau, commission, or other organization that it may select, with the task of carrying out an enquiry or giving an expert opinion." Id., Art. 50. See also Protocol, Arts. 21 and 22.

[26] Protocol on The Code of The Court of Justice (annexed to E.C.S.C. Treaty). Art. 11; See also E.E.C. Treaty, Art. 166.

Applying the Law

The legal issue will be litigated under international law as invoked by the parties, interpreted by the International Peace Court and made reviewable by the designated appellate tribunal.

Guidance in the application of international law to the issue of violence is available in Article 52 (1) of the United Nations Charter, which authorizes the activities of regional agencies for dealing with matters of international peace and security on condition that:

their activities are consistent with the Purposes and Principles of the United Nations.

The Purposes and Principles of the United Nations are set forth in the Charter[27] in part as follows:

The purposes of the United Nations are:
1. To maintain international peace and security, and to that end: to take effective collective measures for the prevention and removal of threats to the peace, and for the suppression of acts of aggression or other breaches of the peace, and to bring about by peaceful means, and in conformity with the principles of justice and international law, adjustment or settlement of international disputes or situations which might lead to a breach of the peace;....

The organisation and its Members... shall act in accordance with the following Principles.
1. The Organisation is based on the principle of the sovereign equality of all its Members.
2. All Members, in order to ensure to all of them the rights and benefits resulting from membership, shall fulfill in good faith the obligations assumed by them in accordance with the present Charter.
3. All Members shall settle their international disputes by peaceful means in such a manner that international peace and security, and justice, are not endangered.
4. All Members shall refrain in their international relations from the threat or use of force against the territorial integrity or political independence of any state, or in any other manner inconsistent with the Purposes of the United Nations....
6. The Organisation shall ensure that states which are not Members of the United Nations act in accordance with these Principles so far as may be necessary for the maintenance of international peace and security.

This is a transcript of community expectations. It is formulated in norms encoded at the highest level of international organization. It articulates the expectation that these norms shall have universal application, even among the few states which are not members of the United Nations. The norms themselves provide a comprehensive spectrum of the community's proscription of unauthorized international violence. Article 1 proscribes violence not just in the most obvious form of "acts

[27] Articles 1 and 2.

of aggression," but in the divers shadings that may be included under "other breaches of the peace" and "threats to the peace."

Standing at the textual level the Charter's norms seem rather abstract. Through the filter of the adjudicative process, however, they will be able to pass from the level of abstraction to the level of concrete meaning.

Illustrative Case

It may be useful to illustrate the way in which these norms may be applied to various forms of violence. As any expression of judgment here upon an actual conflict would give the present study a controversial tone neither necessary to its thesis nor compatible with its spirit of impartiality, a hypothetical case reflecting reality will be offered.

State A and State B are contiguous but not friendly. As part of a program to arm itself with nuclear weaponry, State A conducts an experimental nuclear explosion in the air over its own territory, an act which would be a violation of the Nuclear Test Ban Treaty, if State A were bound by the treaty. The explosion does not result in any fallout over State B's territory. However, it does produce mental apprehension among the population of State B, many of whom demand that their government do something, by force of arms if necessary. State B asks State A to desist from further explosion. State A refuses on the ground that since it did not sign the Nuclear Test Ban Treaty, it is not bound by its terms.

Again State A detonates a nuclear bomb over its own territory, but this time radioactive fallout drifts over State B's territory. State B discovers its milk supply contaminated with strontium 90 from the fallout. State B considers itself to be a victim of unauthorized violence and petitions the Court to condemn the conduct of the government of State A.

The Court holds a hearing and finds the facts as stated. It holds that the acts of State A do not constitute aggression because there is no evidence of a deliberate assaultive intent in State A. As to the first detonation, the Court, recalling the Roman Law maxim, *sic utere tuo ut alienum non laedas* (use that which is yours in a way that will not harm others), holds that State A has committed a threat to the peace by producing in the minds of State B's people a feeling of imperilment that could lead to violent reprisal, even though the act complained of took place over State A's own territory. As to the second detonation, the Court holds that State A has committed a breach of the peace because of the transnational impact and the damage produced in the territory of State B. The Court concludes, therefore, that the government of State A is guilty of unauthorized acts of violence against the security and integrity of State B and against the peace of the community of nations in violation of international law.

The Court's judgment would reflect an interpretation of the norms suggesting that the term "breach of the peace" could properly be applied to action across state borders, while action confined within a border might constitute a "threat to the peace."[28] Views divide around the definition of the term "aggression," but the definitional requirement that the coercive impact be purposive, as suggested hypothetically, would seem consistent with the language of Article 2 (4) of the Charter, "*against* the territorial integrity or political independence of any state..."[29] (Emphasis added.)

An analysis of the judicial response would disclose that the Court is in effect applying the norm of the Nuclear Test Ban Treaty to a state which has not participated in the treaty. The Court would seem to be justified in holding that the state, even though not subject to the Treaty, is, nonetheless, subject to the peace norms of the United Nations Charter, the applicability of which is universalized by Article 2 (6).[30]

Moreover, it is conceivable that the Court could find that the testing prohibition of the Nuclear Test Ban Treaty had come to acquire a status of universal applicability by operation of customary law,[31] in

[28] See Kelsen, *Recent Trends In The Law Of The United Nations* 930 (1951) for a discussion of these terms.

[29] See the summary of definitional approaches in McDougal and Feliciano, *Law And Minimum World Public Order* 61–62, 143–50 (1961). On the definitional requirement of purposiveness see *id.*, p. 64, also p. 175–76 thus:

> The objectivities or subjectivities of participants (or more precisely, of the top effective decision-makers in participating states) cannot ... be wholly disregarded in characterizing coercion as impermissible.

[30] See Falk, *The Authority Of The United Nations To Control Non-Members* (1965). Professor Falk's conclusion, at p. 100, is that:

> Most importantly the issue presented is whether a substantial majority of states in the world may "legislate" for an absent or even a dissenting minority. It would appear, at least on the issue of maintaining the peace, that such legislative competence must be acknowledged in view of the increasing gravity of the threat of war and the growing interdependence of the world communities, as well as the virtually unchallenged exercise of such competence in the practice of the United Nations.

[31] The International Law Commission of the U.N. included the following relevant provisions in its Draft Articles On The Law Of Treaties:

> Article 30
> *General rule regarding Third States*
> A treaty does not create either obligations or rights for a third State without its consent.
> ...
> Article 34

view of the number of states subscribing to the treaty[32] with some conception of it as a legal requirement,[33] and in view of the General Assembly's condemnation of the use of nuclear weapons as a violation of the Charter.[34]

This function of the Court in construing the meaning of norms consistently with any normative definition which may be provided by the Security Council is as consistent with the intent of the framers of the Charter as it is necessary for effective law. It is consistent with their intent in that the framers, by not precisely defining these norms in anticipation of the Security Council's exercise of its primary responsibility, have left their meaning open for future precision.[35] It is a necessary function in that normative precision is essential to adequate compliance, particularly in the grey area where meanings are not obvious, and where resulting disagreement of interpretation undermines the willingness of governments to be bound. "In this borderline area," writes Roger Fisher,

> where a rule of international law is unclear and can reasonably be interpreted in different ways, the very concept of compliance depends upon there being a court or some other authoritative way of determining what the rule is.[36]

> *Rules in a treaty becoming binding through international custom*
> Nothing in Articles 30 to 33 precludes a rule set forth in a treaty from becoming binding upon a third State as a customary rule of international law.

Int. Law Commission, Reports on the second part of its seventeenth session, 3–28 Jan. 1966 and on its eighteenth session, 4 May–19 July, 1966, in Gen. Assembly, *Off. Rec.: Twenty-First Session Supplement No.* 9 (A/6309/Rev. 1) (1966), pages 14–15.

[32] According to U.S. State Dept., *Treaties In Force* 319 (1969), about 98 states have ratified or acceded to the Treaty as of January, 1969.

[33] The following requirements for the emergence of customary international law are offered in Hudson, Excerpt from Working Paper on Art. 24, Stat. Int. Law Commission, U.N. doc. A/CN, 4/16, (3 March 1950), 5, set forth in Briggs, *The Law of Nations* 25 (1952):

> (a) concordant practice by a number of States with reference to a type of situation falling within the domain of international relations;
> (b) continuation or repetition of the practice over a considerable period of time;
> (c) conception that the practice is required by, or consistent with, prevailing international law; and
> (d) general acquiescence in the practice by other States. Of course the presence of each of these elements is to be established ... as a fact by a competent international authority.

[34] See General Assembly Resolution 1653 (XVI), declaring that:

> (a) The use of nuclear and thermo-nuclear weapons is contrary to the spirit, letter and aims of the United Nations and, as such, a direct violation of the Charter of the United Nations;
> (b) The use of nuclear and thermo-nuclear weapons ... is contrary to the rules of international law and to the laws of humanity; ....

See also General Assembly Resolution 1910 (XVIII) taking note of the Test Ban Treaty with approval and calling upon:

> all States to become parties to the Treaty ... and to abide by its spirit and provisions ....

[35] See Report of Rapporteur, Committee 3 to Commission III, 12 *United Nations Conference on International Organization* doc. 881 (English) p. 505; and McDougal and Feliciano, p. 61.

[36] Fisher, "Responding to Disarmament Violations," XVIII *Bulletin of the Atomic*

As rules relating to aggression, breach of the peace and threat to the peace have not been fully predetermined by either Charter or Council, they are susceptible of gradual precision – case by case – through adjudication. An International Peace Court can perform this role.

The Judgment

The judgment is the Court's response to both the factual issue and the legal issue raised by the claim brought before it. After hearing and weighing the evidence for and against the claim, the Court will find that the alleged act of violence across frontiers did or did not occur as a matter of fact. If it finds that the act did occur, the Court will conclude that either it was or it was not authorized as a matter of law.

The judgment will award no compensation. It will pronounce no sentence of physical punishment. But a judgment of censure will constitute an authoritative condemnation of the responsible party. And when the responsible party is the government of a sovereign state this is punishment enough.

The Addressee Of The Judgment

The identification of the responsible party in a matter of this delicacy requires the circumspection that will avoid the risk of assigning guilt by association. Certainly the people of the nation may not be a conscious party to their governments' culpable decision. Both the requirement of justice and the purpose of deterrence call for precise aim in the condemnatory judgment. The principle is implicit in Roger Fisher's counsel:

> For in the case of a government, the people who made the decision in question and the nation against which a punishment be imposed are necessarily different. To the extent that punishment is designed to act as a deterrent to future violations it should be directed at the individual who will in fact be deciding the government's conduct.[37]

Scientists No. 7, p. 22, 27 (1962). See also Barkun, *Law Without Sanctions* 140 (1968):

> The attempt to classify an entire series of incidents under a single magisterial rule makes sense in an American appellate Court but not internationally, where the more portentous and more general the rule the more difficult its correlation with behavioral sources. For this reason the piecemeal solution of small problems through modestly constructed rules is a sounder procedure.

See also Fuller, *The Morality Of Law* 56 (1964):

> In a complex and numerous political society courts perform an essential function. No system of law – whether it be judge-made or legislatively enacted – can be so perfectly drafted as to leave no room for dispute. When a dispute arises concerning the meaning of a particular rule, some provision for a resolution of the dispute is necessary. The most apt way to achieve this resolution lies in some form of judicial proceeding.

[37] Fisher, *id.* p. 26.

Where the culpable governmental decision concerns the perpetration of an act of substantial violence against another nation, it will very likely, of course, be a collective decision, either implicating the policy-making level of the executive branch or implicating the legislative branch of the government, or implicating both branches jointly. A carefully drafted judgment can so specify.

The reason that the people of a state are not to be blamed for the misdeeds of their government, even when they have elected it into office, is that government officials in their day to day decision-making do not act as agents of the people. This was the insight of Edmond Cahn:

> Yet, except in instances of a popular referendum or some other direct vote on a very specific issue, there is no genuine parallel between political representation and legal agency .... Within the limits imposed by decency and fair play, a public official of consequence (for example, a president, congressman, judge, or district attorney) is entitled and obliged to use his own best judgment and do what he concludes congruous with the public interest. As long as he retains his office, he is free to exercise its authority independently.[38]

Concededly this view of official functional independence would not serve, however, to exonerate an electorate which by its silence, or even more, by active adherence, ratifies its government's long standing anti-social policy. It does posit, however, the moral imputability of the decision-makers themselves.

Consistently with this view, it would not appear unreasonable to extend the imputability of the decision-makers directly involved in policy to their associates in government, that is, to those who, though not directly involved in policy formation, do, nonetheless, participate in supporting and executing it. Nor should the defense of superior orders be available to such persons, in keeping with the spirit of Principle IV of the Nurnberg Principles formulated by the International Law Commission pursuant to an authorizing resolution of the General Assembly.[39] Principle IV reads:

> The fact that a person acted pursuant to order of his government or of a superior does not relieve him from responsibility under international law, provided a moral choice was in fact possible to him.[40]

The indictment of an entire nation, recalling Edmund Burke, would be excessive. Conversely, individual accusation would seem deficient,

[38] Cahn, *The Predicament of Democratic Man* 48 (1961).

[39] General Assembly Resolution 177 (II), directing, at paragraph (a), The International Law Commission to:

> formulate the principles of international law recognized in the Charter of the Nurnberg Tribunal and in the judgment of the Tribunal.

[40] International Law Commission, "Report to the General Assembly," II *Yearbook I.L.C. 1950*, p. 375 (1957).

where the judicial task is to assess responsibility for damage caused by the collective force of many united minds which shatter the peace of the world through international violence. For a matter of this enormity the proper party respondent is the responsible governmental collectivity itself.

The Flexible Use Of The Judgment

In view of the severity of the sanction of judicial censure addressed to state parties, particularly as refined by the use of television,[41] and in consideration of the respect which is appropriate to the dignity of states, a dignity attaching to their twofold capacity both as particular communities of people and as major components of the universal community, the power of the sanction should not be applied lightly. A responsible use of this sanction implies that its application be circumscribed by the observance of fair standards of necessity and proportion. When he spoke of the pressure of public opinion upon states summoned before the European Court Of Justice by the executive bodies of the European Communities, Judge A. M. Donner, The President of the Court, uttered a similar admonition:

> Of course, this is not a measure to take every day and it is expected that the executive bodies will be circumspect in using this right.[42]

Circumspection would suggest that judicial censure be used neither before necessity demands it nor beyond what necessity demands at any point in the decision process. It suggests, moreover, the desirability of the graduated response to be drawn from a repertoire of alternative procedural resources made available to the Court's discretion, such as, for example, the devises of suspension of judgment, provisional judgment, final judgment and modification of judgment. The economy and flexibility provided by a range of sanctioning alternatives facilitates a court's creative adaptation of its discretion to varying situational needs. This discretion has a counterpart in national legal systems.[43]

[41] See Friendly and Goldfarb, *Crime and Publicity* Chapter 12 (1967), answering the objection that television coverage in a criminal proceeding would distract participants, inhibit testimony, and degrade dignity. The authors maintain that distraction can be minimized by the hidden camera, that the open testimony will discourage falsification and, at p. 233, that:

> Television could report trials fairly and exactly and with solemnity, just as it has presented other events without any loss of decorum – the British coronation, royal weddings, the Kennedy and Churchill funerals, state visits, medical and scientific accomplishments, serious legislative debates, and the sessions of the United Nations.

[42] Donner, "The Court of Justice of the European Communities," *International and Comparative Law Quarterly, Supp. No. 1*, 66, 71 (1961).

[43] See, e.g., Schmidt and Strömholm, *Legal Values in Modern Sweden* 17 (Stockholm 1964):

The following range of judgmental responses would seem appropriate for an International Peace Court.

1. *Judgment Upon Plea of Guilt.* Where a defendant state prefers to plead guilty in order to avoid a trial, with its attendant exposure of facts and elaboration of issues, the Court could be given discretion to accept such a plea without trial and enter judgment upon it. Where a defendant state has been charged with an offense, such as breach of the peace, and is willing to plead guilty to an offense of lesser seriousness, such as threat to the peace, again the Court could be given discretion to accept such a plea with the consent of the complainant state as an interested party. The advantage of this procedural alternative is that it relieves both parties as well as the Court of the burden and expense of going to trial. It does so without sacrificing the deterrent function of the Court, which is mediated particularly through the judgment itself. While a judgment of lesser severity, in the manner proposed, would appear to lose something of its deterrent impact, this appearance would conceivably be compensated by the unusual feat of eliciting from a government an admission of its own guilt without first having to defeat it.

2. *Suspension of Judgment.* Where the submitted issue of violence involves an ancillary civil issue, such as one of title to territory, the Court may discern that a good prospect for relieving the threat of future violence lies in the separate resolution of the civil issue. To take advantage of this prospect, the Court, in its decretion, may elect to suspend its proceedings pending such outcome upon receiving the consent of the parties to refer the civil issue to the International Court of Justice or other appropriate tribunal for decision. In this instance the Court would be putting its power of judgment to best use by holding it in reserve.

This procedural adjustment would serve the purpose of the Court by providing the accused state with an incentive to reach a resolution of the civil grounds of violence. If a civil settlement were to remove the cause of violence, there would be no necessity to proceed to judicial censure. The threat thereof would have sufficed.

> The wide and variegated range of sanctions leaves considerable scope for the discretion of the courts, a discretion which should be exercised in the light of a thorough examination of the delinquent's personal background.

See also Jones, "Law And Morality In The Perspective Of Legal Realism," 61 *Columbia Law Review* 799, 807 (1961):

> Again, once the criminal defendant has been found guilty, leeway and responsibility characterize the duty of the sentencing judge. The statutory precept, more likely than not, leaves a wide range of permissible treatment of the offender.

3. *Provisional Judgment.* Where a violent episode presages a continuing course of violence for the future, the Court's censuring judgment could be designated provisional, with the proviso that it will be vacated if the adjudged party amends its ways by abandoning its planned course of action and by respecting the independence and territorial integrity of its neighbors during a stated probationary period. At the end of the period there would be an automatic review of the judgment in the light of defendant's interim record. The judgment then would be either vacated or finalized.

The procedure would provide the offender with a *locus poenitentiae,* a place for repentance. The proffered reward of the expunged record would be the incentive for repentance.

The Common Law has its counterpart doctrine of abandonment. It is available in some jurisdictions as a defense to a charge of criminal attempt. One judge defined the doctrine in this way:

> Abandonment is a defense if the attempt to commit a crime is freely and voluntarily abandoned before the act is put in process of final execution and where ther is no outside cause prompting such abandonment.[44]

The present suggestion would depart from the Common Law version in its contemplation of an outside cause prompting abandonment, the outside cause being the Court's reserve power of censure. If by this prompting the defendant state can be induced to abandon its deviant course, then the power of the Court will have served its end without need of being unleashed.

4. *Final Judgment.* The procedural devices of suspended judgment and provisional judgment are graduated responses tailored to special situations by judicial discretion. They engage the Court's reserve power in lieu of its applied power. They are to be invoked both out of respect for the dignity of the defendant state and out of respect for the law of parsimony, which would dictate that less severe measures be exhausted before resort to the more severe.

If these measures are not effective, however, then the ultimate sanction of the judgment of censure could be entered upon the record. Unless later modified for good reason, that judgment would be final – its record permanent.

5. *Modification Of Judgment.* In the interest of justice and effective application of law, it would seem reasonable to provide that any judgment of the Court may be reconsidered upon the discovery either

[44] People v. Von Hecht, 133 California Appeals 2d Series 25, 36; 283 Pacific Reporter 2d Series 764, 771 (1955), White, Presiding Justice.

of new evidence or of fraud in the original proceedings. However, it could be provided that any judgment may, in the Court's discretion, be vacated upon application of the adjudged state supported by a showing of good conduct sustained for a substantial time coupled with reparation of past adjudicated injuries to others. Thus to time's forgetting would be added the forgiveness of the expunged record.

This judicial tact would differ from the procedure for the review of a provisional judgment in that the review here would not be routine. It would be by the grace of the Court upon special application of the adjudged state with commensurate proof annexed. The assessable period of meritorious conduct would likely be set longer for modification after a final judgment than for vacation after a provisional judgment.

Unless thus altered by the Court or reversed on appeal by an appellate tribunal, a final judgment will stand. And out of the judgment will come the impact of the Court.

VII

THE COURT IN IMPACT

The very appearance of an International Peace Court can have an impact on the international environment. The opening of its doors for business may initiate a ripple of new awareness and rising expectation that will move out and spread across that environment to its remotest shores. The operation of the Court may have a further impact on the environment consisting not only of its immediate focal effect in the cases, but, beyond the cases, of some inescapable systemic consequence affecting the legal process implicit in the international order. The precise bounds of such focal effect and systemic consequence must await the measurement of empiric data. Their appraisal, and by consequence appraisal of the Court itself, will come only after the data are in. Until then, the effectiveness of the Court in achieving the results projected for it can be neither accurately predicted nor precluded.

Assessment of the results is for the future. Plausible expectations relating to these results, however, can be given present clarification. More particularly, the hypothesis supporting these expectations can be spelled out in its several terms of environmental reference – physical, psychological, moral and legal. This will be attempted in the following anticipation of the Court's impact by way of its operational effect and, beyond that, by way of its legal consequence.

Operational Effect

It is anticipated that the operational effect of the projected International Peace Court will correspond with its objective, the deterrence of unauthorized violence by states. The basis of the expectation may be questioned: how can a system of public judgment be expected to deter nations from violence? What circuitry of influence will connect the judgment of a court with the subjectivities of governments?

The Circuitry Of Deterrence

The best answer to this question may be to trace the movement set up by the impulse of the judgment of the Court through its expected pathway of influence. The circuit of deterrence will run through a set of physical, psychological and moral factors starting with the moral sentiment of the people.

In the first place, the collective moral sense will support the making of judgment. The judgment will be pronounced from the bench. The pronouncement will inform the parties of the defendant state's transgression. The information will be reproduced in the verbal and the visual message. The message will be carried through the media of communication into the currents of world judgment. There it will deliver an impact on the public image of the adjudged state.[1] Finally, from this information-image complex the sensitive nerve endings of the subjectivities of the condemned violator, as well as of the potential violator,[2] will pick up the message of censure.

Because "every state," as we are reminded, "is extraordinarily sensitive to the mere suspicion of illegal action," [3] the message of censure is freighted with deterrence. The condemned violator senses the stigma of illegality as a present reality. The potential violator senses it as a future possibility.

The Moral Factor

The reason for the observed phenomenon of governmental sensitivity to world judgment would seem to lie in the moral force of the community's resentment and denunciation of violence. The Collective Measures Committee referred to this moral component in its analysis of political sanctioning measures, measures which include the denunciation of an offending state, when it recognized that:

> Such measures must, as a general rule, depend for their effect on moral factors.[4]

[1] The impact will involve attitudinal changes in peoples' expectations and demands in relation to the adjudged state, and in their sense of identity in the face of its assault upon their larger community. Cf. Murty, *Propaganda And World Public Order* 22 (1968).

[2] See Hart, "The Aims Of The Criminal Law," 23 *Law and Contemporary Problems* 401, 426 (1958), in Paulsen and Kadish, *Criminal Law And Its Processes* 130 (1962):

> Punishments should be severe enough to impress not only upon the defendant's mind, but upon the public mind, the gravity of society's condemnation of irresponsible behavior. But the ultimate aim of condemning irresponsibility is training for responsibility.

[3] Brierly, "Sanctions," 17 *Transactions of the Grotius Society* 69–70 (1932).

[4] United Nations Collective Measures Committee, "Report" in General Assembly, *Official Records, Sixth Session, Supp. No. 13* (A/1891) p. 3, section 25 (1951). Cf. Cahn, *The Predicament of Democratic Man* 54 (1961):

> That is why the very utterance of a protest constitutes an act of faith in the popular vindication of right and justice.

The moral factor weighs heavily in the minds of governments. Their apparent willingness to infringe it in deed is sharply contrasted with an apparent unwillingness to deny it in word.

The evidence tends to show that governments, however secure may be their material position, however high their prestige rating, are vulnerable to the sanction of moral disapproval. This vulnerability would clearly seem to be linked with the valuation placed upon good name and reputation in the community, a valuation which in turn may be associated with the fundamental urge to survive felt by both individuals and nations. Kelsen has sought to account for the underlying principle in this way:

> Approval and disapproval by the fellow members of the community are sensed as reward and punishment and may therefore be interpreted as sanctions. Sometimes they are more effective sanctions than other forms of reward and punishment, because they satisfy or hurt man's desire for reputation, which is one of the most important components of the instinct for self-preservation.[5]

The power of moral disapproval is not created by the judgment of a

[5] Kelsen, *Pure Theory of Law* 27–28 (2d rev. ed. 1967, Knight transl.). See also 13 *Encyclopedia of the Social Sciences* 531 (1934), thus:

> The sanctions existing in a community constitute motives in the individual for the regulation of his conduct in conformity with usage. They are effective, first, through the desire of the individual to obtain the approbation and to avoid the disapprobation of his fellows. . . .

Compare Gardiner, "The Purposes of Criminal Punishment," 21 *Modern Law Rev.* 117, 123 (1958):

> This is not to say, however, that deterrence never works. On the contrary, it works very often. But it works less through fear of punishment itself, than through fear of social disapprobation. The majority of people need the approval of their fellow citizens. Consciously or unconsciously, we spend a good deal of time looking over our shoulder to those whose esteem we value.

And Sykes, *The Society of Captives* 67 (Atheneum 1965, Copyright 1958 by Princeton Univ. Press):

> . . . the loss of that more diffuse status which defines the individual as someone to be trusted or as morally acceptable is the loss which hurts most.

The impact of moral disapproval upon nations was observed by Elihu Root, *loc. cit. supra*, Chapter IV:

> It is difficult to say just why such opinion is of importance, because it is always difficult to analyze the action of moral forces; but it remains true and is universally recognized that the nation which has with it the moral force of the world's approval is strong, and the nation which rests under the world's condemnation is weak, however great its material power.

The parallel effect of the moral sanction on the businessman has been noted in Honnold, "The influence of the Law of International Trade on the Development and Character of English and American Commercial Law," in Schmitthoff (ed.), *The Sources Of The Law Of International Trade* 76 (London, 1964):

> The most effective sanction towards contract compliance in most transactions (both foreign and domestic) is the necessity for a trader to preserve his reputation for reliability and business morality . . . . In view of the specialized nature of foreign trade, it has few counterparts of the occasional door-to-door and fly-by-night domestic transaction: making an honourable adjustment usually costs less than the loss of goodwill from dishonour.

court. It can be released and directed, however, through the judgmental catalyst.

Indeed, it is possible that without the refinement and focus of an organized outlet, the gross, amorphous outpouring of moral opprobrium may fall short as a corrective force in international affairs.[6] The profusive odium attaching to the invasion of Hungary in 1956 did not deter the invasion of Czechoslovakia in 1968. The unorganized expression of moral sentiment evidently can remain diffuse and ineffective until it is adjusted to focus upon a determinate unit of conduct, an identified responsible party and a definite norm violated. This is particularly the case where act and actor have to be disentangled from a maze of contradictory assertions of fact and competing claims of right. And the process of disentangling can only be effectively and convincingly done by a rational decision-maker bearing the credentials of the community.

Summary

The Collective Measures Committee has noted the deterrent potential of a determination and denunciation made by an authoritative body such as the Security Council or the Assembly, on the issue of a threat to the peace, in observing that:

> Such determination and denunciation, either by the Security Council or the General Assembly, even if not followed immediately by other collective measures, clearly constitute a strong warning signal, not only for the party or parties concerned but for all other nations.[7]

If determination and denunciation by the Security Council and the General Assembly have this tendency to deter, how much more will determination and denunciation by an impartial international judiciary?

[6] Cf. Taubenfeld, *op. cit.* at 204:

> The myth of the corrective force of international opprobrium which was relied on as a potent deterring force in the post-Victorian world of the League System needs re-examination.

Cf. Mc Dougal and Feliciano at 275, stating that in a sense:

> ... public opinion is the ultimate and indispensable sanction for all law. From this, nonetheless, no necessary conclusion flows that for serving the effectiveness of any particular legal prescription in a concrete situation, exclusive reliance must be placed upon the inscrutable and automatic workings of amorphous opinion and sentiment.

Cf. further Fisher, "Constructing Rules That Affect Governments" in Brennan (ed.), *Arms Control, Disarmament And National Security* 60 (1961):

> The strength of public opinion will further depend upon such factors as how clear it is that there is a rule, how clear it is that the rule applies to this case, and the extent to which the rule is easily understandable and appeals to common sense.

[7] U. N. Collective Measures Committee, *op. cit.* at 5, section 38.

Legal Consequence

Beyond its impact in deterrent fact, the operation of an International Peace Court will have a certain consequence at law. It may be useful to clarify the extent and meaning of this legal consequence insofar as it may be reached for present analysis.

Toward An International Criminal Law

Hopefully, the Court will advance the maturation of international law in pace with the intensifying claims of the evolving global order. Perhaps this anticipated legal advance can best be conceptualized as a move along a continuum stretching from an international tort law to an international criminal law. It may be conceived, in other words, as a development away from the accommodation of differences between nation and nation through reparation by one of past wrongdoing to the other, to a process for the punitive deterrence, by the community, of future wrongdoing by one of its member nations.

Criminal law, thus understood, is underdeveloped in the chronicle of world law. In the early years of this century Professor Oppenheim wrote that: "An international delinquency is not a crime, because the delinquent State, as a Sovereign, cannot be punished, although compulsion may be exercised to procure a reparation of the wrong done."[8] In later editions Oppenheim added qualifying words after the word "punished," to read, "in the same way as a delinquent individual."[9] A still later edition of Oppenheim by Lauterpacht came around to recognizing "violations of international law amounting to a criminal act in the generally accepted meaning of the term."[10] This engaging conceptual sequence was pointed out by Professor Schwarzenberger in an article written in 1950,[11] in which he offered the doctrinal reflection that an international criminal law worthy of the name would have to consist of prohibitive rules endowed with specifically penal sanctions.

Accepting Professor Schwarzenberger's criteria for an international

[8] Oppenheim, 1 *International Law* 201 (1905).

[9] Vol. 1, p. 246 (1920); Vol. 1, p. 291 (1928).

[10] Vol. 1, p. 307 (Lauterpacht ed. 1947); accord Vol. 1, p. 339 (Lauterpacht ed. 1955), and at p. 355 thus:

> The State, and those acting on its behalf, bear criminal responsibility for such violations of international law as by reason of their gravity, their ruthlessness, and their contempt for human life place them within the category of criminal acts as generally understood in the law of civilized societies.

[11] Schwarzenberger, "The Problem Of An International Criminal Law," 3 *Current Legal Problems* 263, 273–74 (1950), in Mueller and Wise (eds.) *International Criminal Law* 3, 13–14 (1965).

criminal law, it would seem reasonable to maintain that the norms of the United Nations Charter in derogation of recourse to aggression, breach of the peace, and threat to the peace are indeed prohibitive. While a penal sanction is not affixed to their violation by the Charter exactly in the manner of a domestic penal code, that is, by express prior notification, these norms would indeed become endowed with a penal sanction through the application of the adjudicatory censure provided in the projected International Peace Court. In this instance prior notification would be implicit in the public installation of the Court. If a sanction is defined as a deprivation of some value employed to support a norm,[12] then the judicial censure of a state government would seem to qualify as a sanction: the deprivation consisting in the loss of the good name and public respect which states tend to value in a special way; the norm being that of the Charter.

Moreover, it would not seem too much to suggest that the impact of such disapproval conveyed by the public censure has something of a specific penal character. Censure by its nature would seem to be penal or painful. It would seem to be necessarily intended to cause pain. Etymology has its clues here. The word "penal" is derivative, through the French, of the Latin word "poena" for "pain." The words "punish and "punitive,"" stem from the Latin word "punire" meaning "to punish," which is a variant of the Latin "poenire", itself an adaptation of "poena." The sanction of public censure, as envisaged here, obviously would not only cause pain, in the form of mental pain; it would issue from an intent that it cause pain.

At the same time the retribution of censure does not stop at pain. Through the medium of pain it seeks to reach and affect the center of responsibility of the offender. Thereby it would convince him of his wrong in the past, that by appreciating its seriousness, he may be moved to choose right for the future. Such a purpose would be built into the censure provided by an International Peace Court. A criminal conviction is by etymology a convincing. It is a communication intended to convince the recipient of his responsibility.

Penal retribution, in this perspective, is employed to cause pain, but not pain for its own sake, as in sadistic torture or revenge. Where the latter is employed primarily in order to gratify the urge of the torturer or the avenger, the former is employed primarily in order to convince the recipient. To convince him means to make him sensitive to his

[12] See, e.g., Arens and Lasswell, *In Defense of Public Order* 14 (1961). For a study of sanctions in depth see Rooney, *Lawlessness, Law and Sanction* (1937).

responsibility for his active choices and their harmful consequences. There may be cases where the offender's sensitivity may be aroused with little or no pain. Hence the importance of flexibility of community response. Hence judicial discretion in setting the sanction.

The effort to convince the offender has a side-effect on the community itself. By providing a channel of expression it averts repression of the community's reaction to the offender, a repression which could breed resentment with its attendant irritations. Repression might also distort the social conscience itself, in the sense that if the expression of community disapproval of wrongdoing is denied, the disapproval itself may disappear.[13]

Used as communication, retribution is rehabilitation rather than requital. So conceived, retributive pain is not sadistic but surgical. This elucidates the purpose of the scalpel of censure. Its cutting edge serves to expose the nerve of moral sensitivity, beyond which may lie the cure. The most reliable deterrent of the offender is his rehabilitation.

Accordingly, collective disapproval addressed to the offender seeks to effectuate a change in his perspective directly, and indirectly a change in his conduct. This constructive function of the public procedure for channeling disapproval, curiously, is accorded scant consideration in the correctional view which would dismiss penal retribution as without productive value. Actually, the communication of disapproval is an implicit act of respect toward the offender. It is a recognition of his dignity as a responsible agent.[14] What is more, it is a recognition of his worth as a potential contributor to the commonweal.[15] Through the punitive symbol, the community demonstrates

[13] Cf. Goodhart, *English Law and the Moral Law* 92–93 (1953):

> It has, therefore, been pointed out that if the criminal law refuses to recognize retributive punishment then there is a danger that people will take the law into their own hands. A far greater danger, to my mind, is that without a sense of retribution we may lose our sense of wrong. Retribution as punishment is an expression of the community's disapproval of crime, and if this retribution is not given recognition then the disapproval may also disappear. A community which is too ready to forgive the wrongdoer may end by condoning the crime.

The question may be asked whether classical international law did not end up condoning generally the harm of war.

[14] Cf. Studt, *A Conceptual Approach To Teaching Materials: Illustrations From The Field Of Corrections* 15 (1965), thus:

> Seldom does the correctional organization manage to provide a basic role for the offenders it serves that defines them as persons of worth who have something to contribute to their society.

[15] Cf. Del Vecchio, *Justice*, 186 (Guthrie transl., Univ. Edinburgh Press, 1952):

> The tendency is thus to respect, not without limits, but certainly to a greater extent than in the past, the personality of the guilty man, which, too, always contains in itself something sacred and cannot be trampled down or denied, even for a supposed equation

that it accepts the responsibility of the latter for his acts and asks that he do the same. A. C. Ewing has noted the therapy implicit in the punitive premise that the offender is responsible for his offense:

> The primary objective of punishment is to lead both the offender and others to realize the badness of the act punished....
>
> We may then regard punishment as a kind of language intended to express moral disapproval.[16]

The characterization of punishment as communication with actual and potential offenders seems particularly appropriate to governments in view of their presumptive lesser susceptibility to the conventional impediments to responsibility: mental illness, ignorance and passion. Despite their aberrations it would still appear that states among the categories of offenders are more accustomed to calculating the effects of their acts. H. L. A. Hart observes that "the old Benthamite confidence in fear of the penalties threatened by the law as a powerful deterrent, has waned with the growing realization that the part played by calculation of any sort in anti-social behavior has been exaggerated" and Abraham Goldstein suspects that "the 'public' is not watching all that closely whose punishment is held up to it by way of example...."[17] But evidently such insights would be more applicable to individual offenders than to governments.

Coming after the offense has occurred, the message communicated by the censure is that it must not occur again. The public adjudicatory context of the communication makes explicit its invocation of community norm. Viewed against these factors the projected procedure of an International Peace Court takes on a criminal cast. It tailors to states a sanctioning modality to which they among all categories of

between the harm done and the harm rendered, without thereby lessening the dignity of those very people who deny it and trample upon it.

See also "Criminals Should Be Cured, Not Caged," 6 *American Criminal Law Quarterly* 138 (Spring, 1968) (Reprinted from Time, copyright Time, Inc. 1968):

> What most convicts really need is neither repression nor sentimental treatment as patients, but rather opportunity for restitution. ....On many occasions, prisoners have fought fire and flood with a zest and courage that amazed and won the communities they saved. As guinea pigs in countless medical experiments, they have voluntarily suffered malaria, cancer, syphilis and other ugly ills for the public benefit – and their own. The key is self-respect: prisons are full of men who perhaps above all need a chance to serve society in order to respect themselves. When the law-abiding public accepts that fact, the U. S. penology will be on the road to genuine rehabilitation.

[16] Ewing, "A Study of Punishment II: Punishment as Viewed by the Philosopher," 21 *Canadian Bar Review* 102, 115–16 (1943).

[17] Hart, *Punishment and Responsibility* 1 (1968); Goldstein, *The Insanity Defense* 13 (1967).

offenders are probably the most susceptible, to wit, the sanction of moral disapproval. It offers a new move toward a penal law for states.

Contrast With The Nurnberg And Tokyo Trials

It might be objected that the move is not new, in that the Nurnberg Trial which condemned the German war criminals following the Second World War and the Tokyo Trial for Japanese war criminals[18] have already consummated an international criminal law. The attractiveness of this conclusion, however, must be tempered by the facts. Both trials were directed to individual offenders, not state governments. (By the same token, the proposed jurisdiction provided in the United Nations Draft Statute For An International Criminal Court[19] extends to "natural persons, whether they are constitutionally responsible rulers, public officials or private individuals."[20] It does not extend to state governments.)

Moreover, even the international character of the jurisdiction exercised by the Four Powers which presided over the Nurnberg Trial is less than unequivocal. As Professor Schwarzenberger observes in his article,[21] both the trial of the German war criminals and the trial of the Japanese war criminals were presided over by occupying powers. Accordingly, the presiding powers in both proceedings can be said to have stepped into shoes of vacated sovereignty and to have proceeded to act in the capacity of co-sovereigns of the respective occupied states. From this circumstance, so interpreted, Professor Schwarzenberger drew the conclusion that, "both these international military tribunals were in substance more akin to municipal war crime courts than to truly international tribunals."[22]

Perhaps some would still prefer to ascribe an international character to the two post-war prosecutions to reflect the fact that they involved nations judging other nations – victors judging vanquished – upon conduct and norms that were international. Nevertheless, the most meaningful question that can be asked about the Nurnberg and Tokyo tribunals from a legal perspective is whether they were constitutionally impartial.

[18] See International Military Tribunal, *Trial of The Major War Criminals*, Vols. 1 to 42 (1947), and U. S. Dept. of State, *Trial Of Japanese War Criminals, Documents* (1946).

[19] See 1953 Committee on International Criminal Jurisdiction, "Report," General Assembly, *Off. Rec., IX, Supp. 12* (A/2645) 23–26 (1954).

[20] *Id.* at Article 25.

[21] Schwarzenberger, *op. cit.* at 290–91, Mueller and Wise at 31.

[22] *Ibid.*

The Qualifications Of A Criminal Tribunal

Professor Schwarzenberger in his article had occasion to recall these words of Lauterpacht:

> It is clear that unless the criminal responsibility of States is to be reduced to the vanishing point of law, its enforcement must be placed in the hands of impartial international agencies operating within the orbit of a politically organized international society.[23]

It is believed that an International Peace Court would meet the Lauterpacht specification as to an impartial international agency. Certainly, unlike the Nurnberg and Tokyo tribunals, the staffing and supporting membership of an International Peace Court would not have the outward color of an antagonist relationship with any accused party. Judges would be selected from the world at large on objective criteria of judicial qualification and cultural pluralism. Membership in the Statute of the Court would be open to all nations without regard to particular relationships with litigant parties. The Court's impartiality, indeed, would be anchored in its internationality.

Furthermore, in keeping with the further stated specification of Professor Lauterpacht, it can be argued with reason that an International Peace Court, as designed herein, would operate within the orbit of a politically organized international society. Its operational framework would be the international society as partially, if primitively, organized in the United Nations. Of the United Nations, C. Wilfrid Jenks has said that: "For the first time in history we have the formal framework of a universal world order and the formal elements of a universal legal order."[24]

Obviously, the political organization represented in the United Nations lacks the sophisticated power complex that some would envision for a world government equipped with a central monopoly of all armed force above the level of local police and militia requirements. For the exercise of the type of power projected in the present design, however, namely moral power, the United Nations in its present general framework could conceivably provide an adequate structural and functional support. If the Court succeeds in its deterrent purpose, there may be neither need nor pressure for a monolithic world government centralizing the regulation of all international processes.

Admittedly, the view of power implicit in this perspective is broad. It has been made explicit by Professor McDougal:

[23] From Oppenheim's *International Law* Vol. 1, p. 323, note 1 (Lauterpacht ed. 1948).
[24] Jenks, *The Common Law of Mankind* 2 (1958).

Bases of power ... include not only naked force, but also the formal authority of governmental position and doctrine and effective control over resources and wealth, enlightenment, respect, skill, well-being and safety, conceptions of right and wrong, and loyalties.[25]

The power of an International Peace Court will be based on the universal demand of governments for the values of respect and reputation for doing right.

Summary

The traditional doctrine of state liability has included recognition of wrongs done by states to other states, recognition of the duty of the former to make reparation to the latter, and recognition of the competence of the latter to assert claims against the former. These features parallel domestic systems in their law of tort or civil responsibility. The operation of an International Peace Court would share some of these features, notably, the recognition of state wrongs and the competence of an aggrieved state to assert a claim. However, there are distinctive features in the projection of an International Peace Court. Of these the following are conspicuous.

1. The claims asserted by aggrieved states would not be for reparations.

2. The assertion of the claims would represent the interests not only of the aggrieved state, but of the community of states. Hence, the Court's procedure could reflect this representative character by providing an option for their assertion by an official agent of the community.

3. The purpose of the assertion of claims would be the public censure of the offender in aid of the offender's deterrent rehabilitation as well as the deterrence of others.

[25] McDougal, "Law and Power," 46 *American Journal of International Law* 102, 108 (1952). See further at p. 111:

> ... the moral goals of people ... are not mere "abstractions" without antecedents or consequences. Such goals are rather the most constructive dynamisms of conscience and character and, when shared with others, are not "sources of weakness and failure," but rather the most dependable bases of power and successful co-operation.

See also Landheer, *On The Sociology Of International Law And International Society* 74 (1966):

> The reality structure of world society is commonly designated as the "power structure," and this is in itself symptomatic, as it indicates the excessive weight that the term "power" has acquired in our thinking. There are many forms of power: spiritual power, the power of knowledge, power of will, physical power, hypnotic power, but "power" has come to mean in the first place the capability of the state to use armed might.
>
> From the point of view of an emerging world society, this power is as atavistic as the club of the caveman, but it is unfortunately the dominant factor in contemporary world society. Perhaps one should see it as a latter-day hypertrophy of an outdated social form which is kept artificially alive by overstressing it.

4. The nature of the wrong redressed by the censure would be public, being a wrong against the whole community rather than a single member thereof.

5. The moral gravity of the wrong redressed is profound, involving jeopardy to the survival of the community.[26]

These distinctive operational features clearly match many of the conventional characteristics which cluster around the criminal label in domestic legal systems.

The presence in the proposed adjudicatory procedure both of features common to tort law and other features associated with criminal law have suggested the model of a tort-crime continuum. The greater number of distinctive criminal-type features will tend to locate the envisaged operation of an International Peace Court nearer the criminal pole of the continuum.

However, the operation will stop short of the full panoply of domestic criminal law, which typically would include features such as the provision for physical techniques for acquiring judicial control over those who are suspected or accused, and the provision for physical and economic methods of execution against those who are convicted. This operational contrast is an inevitable corollary of the structural difference in the organization of power between domestic society and international society.

Professor Lauterpacht has noted that:

> There are no international judicial decisions laying down and applying the principle of criminal responsibility of States. This is largely due to the absence of international tribunals endowed with the requisite jurisdiction.[27]

It is submitted, therefore, that the legal impact of an International Peace Court will be represented in a move along the continuum of international law from the pole of tort or civil responsibility toward the pole of criminal responsibility. Whether the move will be far enough to elicit universal concurrence in applying to it the appellation "criminal law" is a question which need not be answered here.

Ultimately, the consequence of the operation of the Court for the

[26] As distinguished, for example, from the infractions of the norms governing economic integration in the European Common Market for which member states can be censured by the European Court of Justice pursuant to E.C.S.C. Treaty, Art. 88, and E.E.C. Treaty, Art. 169. Such infractions probably would not be regarded as criminal. They are not characterized by the obvious moral turpitude associated with acts of transnational violence. It would seem, therefore, that while all censure is probably painful, all censure is not necessarily criminal.

[27] Oppenheim 356 (Lauterpacht ed. 1955).

development of international law probably will not be best understood by the choice of juristic label. It can better be appreciated in an analysis of the various premises which will enter into service as the conceptual anchorage of the Court in action. Considered together these premises may provide the theory for a breakthrough in a move toward world law.

VIII

NEW PREMISES FOR A LEGAL BREAKTHROUGH

The plan for an International Peace Court presented herein is a new departure from old ways of thinking about the question of how to maintain peace and security in the world. Perhaps it would be more accurate to say that it is a departure not so much from customary thinking as from customary non-thinking, that is, from ways of maintaining underlying premises for positions without articulating these premises or perhaps even adverting to them.

Among these premises are the following:

1. The premise that if the great powers fail to take the initiative against the menace of international violence, then the other nations of the world are powerless to take the initiative;

2. The premise that the only significant bases of influence in the international community are military, economic and diplomatic resources;

3. The premise that the power of moral judgment cannot be harnessed for application to the concrete problems of power relationships between state governments;

4. The premise that the international conduct of a national government may not, without its consent, be subjected to the judgment of a court of law; and

5. The premise that the basis for the effective application of international law ought to be modelled on the basis of effective application in domestic law, i.e., physical enforcement.

In the following pages each of these stereotypes will be considered and contrasted with a proposed new premise. The new premises are a distillate of the other chapters. Placed together they form a theoretical foundation for the projected construction.

First Premise: The Initiative of the Many

Old Premise:

That if the great powers fail to take the initiative against the menace of international violence, the other nations are powerless to take the initiative.

The proposed departure from this premise is to move the search for peace and security outside the groove of dependence upon the expectation of unanimity among the few major powers. Within the present constitution of the community of nations, the failure of agreement by the few is not a decree of immobility for all the others. Article 24 of the United Nations Charter simply says that the "Members confer on the Security Council primary responsibility for the maintenance of international peace and security...." It does not say that the members agree to relinquish all responsibility to the Council. Article 51 recognizes their responsibility even to the extent of an inherent right of collective self-defense against armed attack pending exercise of the primary responsibility – "until the Security Council has taken measures necessary to maintain international peace and security."

Indeed, the entrustment of even this primary responsibility to the Council is not without strings attached. Its exercise is tied, by the language of the grant, to the pursuit of a single objective – "to ensure prompt and effective action by the United Nations...."

The terms of the grant, manifestly, are not an authorization to any member of the Council to use its position in the Council to advance its particular interests. The members have been given the authority to represent the interests of the community. Hence, they bear a fiduciary relationship to the community. According to the terms of the grant, the conferring members – "agree that in carrying out its duties under this responsibility the Security Council acts on their behalf."

If the Security Council, in carrying out its duties under the responsibility conferred by the world's nations, acts on their behalf, it would seem to follow that, whenever it fails to carry out its duties under this responsibility, it fails to act on their behalf. In the event, therefore, that the Council fails to act on behalf of the nations to ensure prompt and effective action to protect international peace and security, it would seem to follow that the nations of the world must assert their residual responsibility for the maintenance of peace and security.

Of old a significant hold on the channels of international influence rested with a few major powers. It was then expected that these powers would take the initiative in international affairs, and that the other nations would follow. This expectation has been altered. The international caste system of leaders and followers is coming loose. The little powers are graduating from their former tutelage. Rather than look to their old preceptors for their thinking, they are advancing thoughts of their own. They are heard sharing the same media of communication as the major powers, where they match the major powers' proposals with proposals of their own. It is a two-way dialogue.

Through this dialogue, the generality of states are showing that they expect not just to be influenced, but to influence. They are making motions like first class participants in the decisions that determine the future of the community. International participatory democracy is evolving in the assembly of man.

The larger body of nations seem to hope that their more advantaged neighbors will use their affluence and their influence not for exclusive ends but for stewardship. Their concept of cooperation seems less a matter of dependency, and more a matter of shared respect and shared responsibility.

This residual responsibility of the larger community of nations is not a bare formal title. It is conjoined with access to resources of great potential for effective impact. As the constitution of this community has evolved so as not to exclude the many from all responsibility for the maintenance of peace and security, just so the resource position of the community has evolved in such a way as not to give to the few a monopoly of effective influence.

New Premise

The authority structure of the international community has not been designed to exclude the greater part of its members from communal responsibility and initiative for peace. Nor, by the same token, does the resource structure of the community exclude them from the exercise of this responsibility and initiative.

Second Premise: Moral Power as a Base of International Influence

Old Premise:

That the only significant bases of influence in the international community are military, economic and diplomatic resources.

If the only base of influence in the international community were material power, the vast majority of nations might perhaps have to settle for a nominal role of participation in the crucial decision making process of their community. One significant base of influence, however, should not be overlooked in surveying the resource position of this planetary community, and that base of influence is the people who make it up. Access to military and economic power they may not have, most of them, but what they do have is the power of moral censure. And this is a power which, if released and channeled, can reach any violator and penetrate the shield of any material defense.

One might suppose in theory that the power of moral censure is crippled as an instrument of influence by the inability of people, particularly people of varying national and cultural backgrounds, to agree upon the specifics of human behavior which ought to be made the object of moral censure. The phenomenon is, however, that as to the specific behavior of international violence, the people of nearly all nations have manifested formal agreement that it is wrong for any state to commit an act of aggression, to cause a breach of the peace, to create a threat to the peace, or to detonate an atomic explosion in the air, under the water or out in space.

Even after formal agreement on general norms, nevertheless, the power of moral sentiment may remain diffuse and its response to the particular transgression mute before the uncertain sound of factual charge and countercharge, of legal claim and counterclaim. The moral power of the community must be called forth by the clarion of definitive decision. Harnessed by legal decision, moral power will be transformed into community judgment.

New Premise

Military, economic and diplomatic resources are not the only significant bases of influence. The international community holds a potentially significant, largely untapped, reserve of influence in the moral judgment of its people.

Third Premise: Moral Power Harnessed to Legal Structure

Old Premise:

That the moral power of the people cannot be harnessed for application to the concrete problems of power relationships between national governments.

On the contrary, if the moral power of the people is connected with an effective channel of application it can prove a potent source of influence in a world of governments. The potential of this influence has already been amplified through the articulation of the norms against violence in the United Nations Charter and the Nuclear Test Ban Treaty, an articulation which has gathered and distilled the moral sentiment of nearly all peoples into criteria for the judgment of international violence.

The way to connect the moral power of the people with an effective channel of application is to provide it with an instrument of focus for exposing and judging facts of international behavior and an instrument of communication for transmitting that which has been exposed and judged. The instrument of communication is already available in the media of electronic transmission.

Moral judgment has often lacked impact because of disagreement on the meaning of norms and confusion on the existence of facts concerning their violation. An International Peace Court can meet this lack by providing an authoritative channel for the interpretation of norm and the authentication of fact. Such a Court will give focus to moral power by replacing the blurred claims of interested parties with the definitive judgment of disinterested judges. The instrument of focus can be fashioned in an International Peace Court.

The modern instrument of communication will make possible the universal transmittal of judgment – both horizontally, in reaching across borders to centers of government, and vertically, in reaching down from governments to their citizenries, reaching even those whose only message from the world outside their village comes to them over a transistor radio. The capability of electronic communication to break through the barriers of space and time renders it a potent instrument for making present to all the act of judgment that can galvanize the power of moral pressure.

New Premise

An international Peace Court will harness moral power to legal structure.

Fourth Premise: Legal Judgment Free of the Consent of the Adjudged

Old Premise:

That the conduct of a national government may not, without its consent, be subjected to judgment by a court of law.

It may be conceded that some special deference is appropriate to national governments under the vague rubric of sovereignty. In certain respects they are and must be more self-directing than other social entities. To be self-directing, however, is not necessarily to be above the judgment of the community. Certainly, the status of sovereignty need not entail the license to jeopardize the interests of the community with impunity. Is not the privilege of sovereignty balanced by the responsibility of sovereignty? Has not a one-sided concept of the privilege in practice evoked the complementary concept of its abuse? In being asked to respect the former concept the people of the international community might well have reservations about the need to respect or tolerate the latter. An immunity from legal process, which may have been consonant with earlier conditions of comparatively limited governmental access to physical power and resulting capability for international disruption, has, through the evolution of weaponry, become a luxury the international community can hardly afford to maintain for any of its members. It would be a perverse ethos indeed which would hold that the physical engine of destruction is all right but that the legal machinery to control it is all wrong.

The idea of an International Peace Court challenges the hallowed anomaly in the law which has suffered the association of the greatest capacity for destruction, i.e. governmental capacity, with the least amenability to judgment. A Peace Court will end the anachronism of immunity and leave governments as answerable for violent behavior as are other parties of lesser destructive capacity. The Court will legalize the adjudgment of governments through a fair procedure organized by their professional peerage.

The proposal projects a departure from a tradition of resigned acquiescence in the non-justiciability of international violence. It seeks to radicalize international law out of the archaic premise that any judicial exercise of jurisdiction over the issue of a state's conduct is subject to the state's consent. In effect it puts the community to an election between the rule of immunity and the law of survival.

New Premise

The people of the world may not be able to procure a state's consent to desist from violence. They do not need a state's consent, however, to lay its act of refusal to desist from violence before the bar of justice.

Fifth Premise: The Unique Method of Implementation of International Law

Old Premise:

That the methodology of effectiveness in international law ought to emulate the methodology of effectiveness in domestic law.

There is the vague uneasy feeling that an effective international law should follow the model of effective enforcement proper to domestic law. The ineffectiveness of international law is commonly attributed to its lack of capacity for physical enforcement, expressed in terms of the absence of a world police force.

However, the role of physical enforcement in domestic law does not provide an appropriate parallel for international law, since the legal ordering of private parties is not the same thing as the legal ordering of governmental entities. In domestic law the fact that some private parties who violate the law either are willing to hazard the stigma of public censure, or else believe they have a fair expectation of avoiding detection, apprehension or conviction, precludes exclusive reliance on a mere judgment of guilt (without punitive sequelae) as a deterrent technique. Since such persons are not to be deterred by the fear of moral censure alone, they must be restrained by other means available either through the application, or through the prospect of the application, of physical incapacitation. But even in domestic law the role of physical enforcement should not be overstated. The compliance of many, particularly of the more responsible members of the community, may be founded as much on concern about the prospect of moral obloquy for non-compliance, as it is on concern about the prospect of physical attachment of their person or property. Merchants, for example, will almost always pay judgments against them before a sheriff seizes their property, because they want to avoid the disgrace and discredit of the unpaid judgment outstanding.

The hardened domestic offender, however, and the governmental offender differ markedly in their fear of judgment. Unlike such individual offenders, a government, by reason of its dual role of internal responsibility in its own country and external responsibility in the company of other governments, cannot afford to be oblivious to public censure. This contrast in subjectivities underlines the greater susceptibility of the governmental offender to the moral sanction.

A further difference is operational. Physical enforcement has an assurance of success in domestic law, where the usual preponderance of physical competence clearly favors the enforcer over the offender, that it does not have in international law, where a favorable preponderance of physical competence on the part of any existing international enforcing agency is less than clear, at least in the case of enforcement against a powerful government.

Finally, detection itself offers a ground of distinction between domestic and international enforcement. The domestic offense is usually clandestine, being produced on a small scale. By contrast, the transnational offense is usually a public spectacle, being staged on a grand scale with a cast of many actors, a theater of operations involving a frontier and at least two countries, and a population-size audience. Even though the production of the transnational offense is typically public, nonetheless, it requires the attendance of a bench of professional critics, of qualified judges, to unravel its plot and significance from its sound and fury.

A comparison in the two levels of legal enforcement, accordingly, brings into contrast the amenability of private individuals to the physical sanction with the amenability of governments to the moral sanction.

Like individuals, law-breaking states customarily do not deny the existence of law. Unlike individuals, however, such states are subject to no impartial application of law to their conduct. They are able to avoid effective community judgment of their excesses by exploiting the consequent imprecisions of norm and fact. They find aid and comfort in the absence of a forum of authoritative adjudication. The certainty of avoiding impartial judgment is their ultimate security.

New Premise

The world community's immediate need for physical enforcement in emulation of domestic law thus seems less clearly established than its need for an authoritative procedure to overcome the exploitation for coercive ends of normative and factual uncertainty in international law. It is for meeting this legal exigency that the international community may well look to the accumulated judicial experience of domestic law as a prototype for an effective international procedure in fact-finding and judgment.

When the results of the experiment are in, they may show that it is the certainty of judgment which will provide governments with their most compelling incentive for compliance with the law of peace and security.

Summary

The idea of an International Peace Court projects something more than a superficial impact on the existing international legal establishment. Its thrust is upon underlying premises. The envisaged effect can be summarized as a shift from formal or ceremonial democracy to actual participatory democracy in the international community's exercise of its residual responsibility for maintaining peace and security.

But the change does not just affect the question of the participants in the process. It extends to the strategy that they may use. The strategy appropriate for use by a broad-based participant constituency of many nations can be expected to differ markedly from a strategy proper to the few. The many should do that which they can do best. Their forte is not material power but moral power.

The strategy of the exercise of moral power is not just the most economic for those on the giving end of peace maintenance. It is also the most effective for the one on the receiving end of the process – the offender state – in view of the peculiar sensitivity of states to moral pressure. An International Peace Court would channelize this power, helping it to reach its target with optimal convergence.

By bringing judgment upon the peace violator without the latter's consent, the Court would in effect overturn the outmoded dogma of sovereign unaccountability.

Accountability in the area of violence will take nothing from peace-loving nations. They have nothing to lose but their insecurity. The impact of an International Peace Court will leave the general legal structure intact while breaking through assumptions which are as anachronistic as they are dangerous.

The breakthrough will open the way for a move ahead toward security through world law.

IX

MAKING THE MOVE

In the foregoing pages the attempt has been to visualize an International Peace Court. In the following pages the concern is to realize the Court, to make it a reality. This involves both establishing the Court and arranging for its maintenance. Establishment will provide the Court with personnel, place to operate and operating procedure. Maintenance will provide for their upkeep.

Establishment of the Court

The establishment of an International Peace Court will be a move by a number of nations which support the objectives of the Court, which share a common perspective on their role of responsibility for the advancement of world law, and which have agreed on a common strategy for the exercise of this role through creation of the Court.

A Common Perspective

The common perspective required to motivate the establishment of the Court can reasonably be expected to proceed from the awareness on the part of many nations that the system of international law which has been inherited from the past provides, as some put it modestly, "no automatic congruence between the community's stake and the effective scope of common authority." [1] The requisite common perspective can also be expected to stem from a consciousness on the part of the participants of the formal legal equality of their membership in the world community under the authority of the United Nations Charter.[2] Some may see more rhetoric than realism in the Charter's acknowledge-

[1] McDougal, Lasswell and Vlasic, *Law and Public Order In Space* 161 (1963).

[2] See U. N. Charter, Art. 2, para. 1:

The Organization is based on the principle of the sovereign equality of all its Members.

ment of its many members' sovereign equality. And, indeed, in the context of material power they are not equal. But in the context of their jural competence, relevant here, they are basically equal.

Luis Padilla Nervo of Mexico, Justice of the International Court of Justice, captured the perspective very well in these words:

Up to now, a small state did not take part in the elaboration of rules and principles of international law. The law of nations was many times the law of powerful nations. Many of those laws are now obsolete and should be revised with the participation of all states, weak or strong, through multilateral agreement and international forums of the United Nations or in international conferences of universal membership in which each state would have equal rights.[3]

This perspective is new without being visionary. It is within the reach of most peoples. It is being encountered in varying expressions and with increasing frequency in the expanding process of international dialogue, such as in the deliberations of the Disarmament Committee convening in Geneva.

It has been heard in sounds of dissatisfaction with the lip-service of dedication to measures for the implementation of international peace and security. Lord Chalfont, the representative of the United Kingdom to the Disarmament Committee noted this development with his endorsement:

The non-aligned States here, and others at various times and with varying degrees of emphasis, have called for measures which would curtail the armament of the nuclear Powers as a price for agreeing to sign a non-proliferation treaty. Their aim, to exert pressure on the nuclear Powers *to match their words with deeds*, is one which in spite of my country's position as a nuclear Power I share wholeheartedly.[4] (Emphasis added.)

The new perspective has been heard in the questioning of a world regulatory mechanism kept up by the balancing of costly military deterrence systems which preempt the resources which could free underdeveloped nations from hunger, disease, ignorance and inhuman misery. Mr. Correa da Costa, the representative of Brazil to the Disarmament Committee made the point:

It is unquestionable that the super-Powers have at their disposal a capacity for nuclear strike many times superior to their security needs – the "overkill" in the disarmament jargon. Why then could we not examine the possibility of converting at least part of those tremendous surpluses of energy to purposes of development? Why should we not transfer to the nuclear and spatial age the biblical appeal to "beat swords into ploughshares"?[5]

[3] From Center for the Study of Democratic Institutions, "Report on Pacem In Terris II," *The Center Magazine* 58 (Oct., Nov. 1967).

[4] ENDC, PV 288, p. 10, Feb. 23, 1967.

[5] ENDC, PV 297, p. 16, May 18, 1967. See also Brazilian Representative Azeredo da Sil-

When the central issue is put to them, is it unrealistic to expect that most nations will register a vote of no confidence in the attitudinal system that tells armed states not to inflict violence on others, but guarantees that if they do so, they shall not be embarrassed by the judgment of an impartial court of law?

To ask them to vote for an International Peace Court is not to make an extravagant demand upon either their trust or their resources. It is, after all, a rather limited proposal asking for very little change of position. The strategic advantage of this fact has been pointed out by a group of researchers in the field of arms control:

> A limited proposal is more likely to find participants who have a common interest in making it effective, and common interest can be carefully nurtured once the beginning has been made.[6]

A Common Strategy

The use of the multilateral agreement called for by Justice Nervo of the International Court of Justice has also been called for by the Chief Justice of the United States. Speaking at the World Peace Through Law Conference in Geneva, in the summer of 1967, Chief Justice Earl Warren envisioned the goal of an international law that will move serious disputes that cause war "into courthouses and away from battlefields." [7] The strategy he recommended for this purpose was treaty-making.[8]

The instrument which was used to constitute the International Court of Justice was a multilateral treaty, The Statute of the International Court of Justice.[9] The same type of instrument can be used to

veira, ENDC, PV 293, p. 11, March 14, 1967 (quoting PV 244, pp. 16–17):

> Why do not the nuclear Powers, along with the treaty, commit themselves, through a declaration of intention, to carrying out a programme based on the following points: first, to take "tangible steps to halt the nuclear arms race and to limit, reduce and eliminate the stocks of nuclear weapons and the means of their delivery" (ENDC/158); second, to stop all nuclear weapons tests – both measures to be taken under adequate international control; third, to increase co-operation with the non-nuclear Powers with a view to accelerating their utilization of nuclear energy for peaceful purposes; and fourth, to channel to the developing countries at least part of the savings effected by the aforementioned disarmament steps?

6 Stanford University, Hoover Institution (research team), "Arms Control for the Far East," *Stanford Today*, Spring 1967, p. 7.

7 Warren, "Inaugural Address," in World Peace Through Law Center, *World Peace Through Law, The Geneva World Conference* 42 (1969).

8 See *id.* at 41:

> Instead of matching each other, soldier for soldier, plane for plane, bomb for bomb and missile for missile, let us create a new kind of competition, a new kind of rivalry, let us match each other law for law, treaty for treaty, until all contacts and relationships in the world community are covered with law....

9 Technically, the Court was established by the U. N. Charter and "constituted ... in accordance with the provisions of the present Statute." Stat. I.C.J., Art. 1.

constitute an International Peace Court. In the evolution of modern international law, the treaty, by becoming multilateral, has been promoted from the role of bilateral contractual instrument to the role of constitutive instrument of international organizations and source of international law.[10] In short, it provides a grass-roots movement in international lawmaking.

The proposed treaty may be designated the Statute of the International Peace Court.

Maintenance of the Court

The proposed Statute of the International Peace Court may constitute the Parties to the Statute as the supporting institution of the Court.

The supporting institution should be open for participation by all nations which endorse its objectives. Its function will be not just to establish, but to maintain the Court. Maintenance will involve the ongoing physical and fiscal support for all phases of the Court's operation, including persons, place and procedure.

Persons

Personnel will include the members of the bench and their administrative staff. The bench might consist of from seven to fifteen judges, the respective quotas of the European Court of Justice and the International Court of Justice, as appropriate for assuring competence and impartiality combined with broad cultural and geographic representation. The Statute might provide that selection of judges be entrusted to the Parties to the Statute, and that judges and their staff be remunerated by the Parties to the Statute through a common fund set up for the financial control of all operations of Court maintenance.

Place

As a center of global communication the place occupied by the Court

[10] See General Assembly, *Official Records, Twenty-first Session, Sixth Committee*, pp. 21–22, wherein the larger role of the multilateral treaty, in contrast with a purely contractual role, is reported to have been noted by the Representative of Brazil, Mr. Amado, October 6, 1966:

> Furthermore, aware of the increasingly important role played by multilateral conventions and the ever-growing tendency to regard them as an important source of international law, the Commission had been able to free that type of instrument from a whole set of outmoded ideas concerning the role of the "parties" – ideas that derived from a purely contractual conception of the treaty.

will provide both function and symbol. Functionally it will be a seat of judgment. Symbolically it will be a house of peace. For both the function and the symbol an appropriate setting for the Court would be Geneva, Switzerland. Just as the city of Geneva provides a convenient center of intergovernmental dialogue and cooperation, so the country of Switzerland enjoys an immemorial association with the ideal of peace between nations.[11]

Procedure

The Court will serve universal peace by providing a competent impartial forum for nation and community beset by international violence. The operational standards deemed necessary to insure minimal impartiality in the discharge of this important function can be summarized from the previous discussion of the Court in action:

a) In order to insure that no grievance or explanation will go unheard, the Court will recognize the standing of any state to appear either on its own behalf or on behalf of another aggrieved state; in a case in which the Parties to the Statute espouse the cause of an aggrieved state, the Court may recognize an appointed surrogate complainant;
b) In order to insure oversight by the universal community, all hearings will be public and all decisions will be published with supporting reasons;
c) In order to facilitate appeals of decisions, advance submission to appropriate appellate jurisdiction will be required of complainant parties, at the option of their respective defendant parties.

Rule Making

The creation of operational specifications in implementation of the proposed function and standards may be allocated partly to the constitutional responsibility of the framers of the Statute and partly to the rule-making responsibility of the judges of the Court. In addition to the guidelines suggested earlier in the discussion of the Court in action, models of judicial design are available in the organic treaties of the two international tribunals principally discussed herein, the International Court of Justice and the Court of Justice of the European Communities, as well as in the proposals contained in the Draft

[11] Mueller in Mueller and Wise (eds.), *International Criminal Law* (1965):
Switzerland is the country of peace, of international understanding, of the conference table, of law abidance and of practiced tranquility among different nationality gro ups.

Statute For An International Criminal Court,[12] itself a synthesis of judicial experience adapted to the prosecution of natural persons for international crimes. Further, the European Convention for the Protection of Human Rights and Fundamental Freedoms is distinguished for its procedural standards relating to accused persons.[13]

Selected provisions of these instruments have been adapted for a suggestive organic treaty for an International Peace Court. Entitled a Model Statute For An International Peace Court, it is presented in the Appendix.

The range of the pertinent specifications can be anticipated to cover the following needs not already discussed in detail.

Judicial Administration

Rules will be required to provide for the number of judges, the method of their nomination and election, their terms of office, their privileges and immunities from personal judicial process, their disability and disqualification, and for the Court officers, including President, Registrar, possibly Court Advocates, and others.

Forensic Proceedings

Rules will be required to provide for pleading in the nature of complaint and answer, notice to the accused party, judicial quorum and

[12] U. N. Committee on International Criminal Jurisdiction (1953), "Report" in General Assembly, *Off. Rec., IX, Supp. 12* (A/2645) 23–26 (1954).

[13] See 213 U.N.T.S. (signed at Rome, Nov. 4, 1950) 221, 228 (1955), Article 6:

(1) In the determination of his civil rights and obligations or of any criminal charge against him, everyone is entitled to a fair and public hearing within a reasonable time by an independent and impartial tribunal established by law. Judgment shall be pronounced publicly but the press and public may be excluded from all or part of the trial in the interests of morals, public order or national security in a democratic society, where the interests of juveniles or the protection of the private life of the parties so require, or to the extent strictly necessary in the opinion of the court in special circumstances where publicity would prejudice the interests of justice.

(2) Everyone charged with a criminal offence shall be presumed innocent until proved guilty according to law.

(3) Everyone charged with a criminal offence has the following minimum rights:

(a) to be informed promptly, in a language which he understands and in detail, of the nature and cause of the accusation against him;

(b) to have adequate time and facilities for the preparation of his defence;

(c) to defend himself in person or through legal assistance of his own choosing or, if he has not sufficient means to pay for legal assistance, to be given it free when the interests of justice so require;

(d) to examine or have examined witnesses against him and to obtain the attendance and examination of witnesses on his behalf under the same conditions as witnesses against him;

(e) to have the free assistance of an interpreter if he cannot understand or speak the language used in court.

voting, publicity of hearings and privacy of deliberations, separate opinions by way of dissent or concurrence, pronouncement of judgments, and revision of judgment.

Due Process Safeguards

Rules will be required to provide for the presumption as to innocence, the quantum of proof required for an inculpating judgment, the burden of proof, the right of attendance, the right to counsel, the rights of interrogation of witnesses and of inspection of evidence.

Guidance in providing for these procedural needs may be suggested by the articles of the Model Statute For An International Peace Court assembled in the Appendix.

Summary

The making of an International Peace Court calls for a grassroots movement of many nations having a common mind and putting their signature to a common set of provisions.

Provided with the personnel, the place, and the procedure, the Court will come into being and will be ready to open its doors to its first case.

And the community of nations will have made a move toward world law.

X

TOWARD WORLD LAW

Blessed are the Peacemakers[1]....

We observe that the persons beatified by Jesus in the Sermon on the Mount are not just the peace-lovers but the peace-makers, those practical idealists who do something to achieve peace.

Nearly everyone loves peace. Even the armed robber prefers peace. He would rather get his victim's money without having to shoot him for it. Even Hitler preferred peace. He would have preferred to annex his neighbor's lands without firing a shot. It is easy to love peace.

It is not easy to make peace. It is not a solution to the problem of international violence to profess a love for peace without doing something about it. And it is not enough to do something about it without doing something responsive to, and commensurate with, the force which impels the violence.

Making Peace

As this force toward violence proceeds from the minds of men, the present design for action directs its thrust upon the process of decision-making that issues in war and other forms of violence. It seeks a commensurate influence upon the minds of responsible international decision-makers in the leverage of judicial power confected in an International Peace Court.

The creation of an International Peace Court has been projected as a grassroots movement. The movement has been seen as a broad-based response to the challenge of international violence so ineffectively confronted by the present institutional arrangement, which has formal responsibility and potential influence but not the requisite common

[1] Matthew 5:9 (Revised Standard Version 1946).

perspective. In place of the shattered perspective of the few most influential nations, the projected effort would engage the shared perspective of the generality of nations.

Two operating requirements have been seen to attach to this grassroots enterprise – resources and authority; resources to make it effective, authority to make it legal.

Resources available to the generality of nations fall far short of the military and economic power of the few major nations. But what the non-major nations do have is the moral power of the people, the constellation of their dedication to peace and development, their moral sense and their access to the channels of new electronic communication. On the policy of promoting that which their resources permit them to do best, the enterprise has been designed to harness this moral power to the deterrence of the governmental criminal intent. The central premise is that the governmental mind is sensitive to moral power when it is applied. In the present design moral power is applied by way of concentration through the judicial process and dissemination through the communication process. The out-put of this dual process will be the legal judgment of censure broadcast to the world.

Authority at the global level is currently loosely organized, at least for the purpose of confronting the challenge of international violence. However, the looseness of the world community's authority structure which contributes to the problem of ineffective control of violence, has the compensatory effect of supporting the authoritative status of the proposed Court. A rigidly organized world structure might have precluded an innovating judicial process. The virtue of the present looseness is in its licensure of innovation. Not only is there no normative preclusion of the new medium, there is positive encouragement, in the form of authorization for international tribunals generally, and particularly for those arrangements in dealing with international peace and security which are assembled on a less than universal base of support. Nevertheless, the new proposal directly challenges an old convention: the immunity of sovereignty from legal judgment. It sees in this privilege a luxury which the community can no longer afford. This challenge may disquiet some vested interest, but it should disquiet no peacemaking nation. It is submitted that the removal of the privilege will not result in the collapse of the legal structure.

And so through the interstices of present legal formality appears the vision of an International Peace Court.

Community Acceptance

The acceptability of the envisioned effort for peace is grounded not just on the evidence of legitimacy, but also on the promise of economy. The outlay demanded of prospective supporters is modest in all categories: in manpower, in resource, in trust and in the moderation of sovereignty. The time required for implementation is not attendant upon the wait for major power accord. Some might feel more comfortable with a more complicated plan of action. But, as the Nobel scientist, James Watson, said after a memorable research breakthrough in deciphering the genetic code:

> Worrying about complications before ruling out the possibility that the answer was simple would have been damned foolishness.[2]

The case for the present proposal finally rests, however, in the prospect it opens for effective peacemaking through lawmaking.

Making Law

It is not possible to chart the course in world legal development that will follow upon the step being proposed here, but it is not too difficult to anticipate certain specific ways in which an International Peace Court can move the world toward law.

The Court can advance world law by ventilating grievances. Is not the history of transnational hostilities explainable in part by the absence of the safety-valve of a forum for venting resentment at trespasses and for giving the satisfaction of an impartial decision? Resort to material power is not the answer to such resentment. Rational judgment is.

The Court can advance world law by giving concrete meaning to abstract legal norms against violence, thereby clarifying the borders of permissible conduct. As norms are thus made more clear, their breach will become more obvious, more difficult to get away with.

The Court can advance world law by shaping community expectations.[3] The people will come to shed their dissociation of international violence from law. They will come to expect legal intervention in state delinquency.

And yet the Court will advance world law more through the antici-

[2] Watson, *The Double Helix* 51 (1968).

[3] See Cahn, *The Sense of Injustice* 33 (1949):

> Through summation of past dispositions as the current law, rules create psychological values of belief, faith, and security....

pation of its judgment than by the number of times it may have to intervene. Moreover, the anticipation of judgment will affect more than the immediate parties to a situation of violence. The risk of association with an impermissible exercise of violence will cause major nations to think twice before assisting in a local conflict. A major state conceivably would find reasons for not risking complicity in the crimes against peace which might later be imputed at law to a client state which is engaging in violence. The awesome concept of international criminal complicity, after all, has been familiarized by the International Law Commission.[4]

The risk of criminal complicity, compounded with the pressure of rising expectations concerning the legal answerability of governmental conduct, may weigh so heavily against the subjectivities of major governments as to incline them to perceive that the policy of fighting each other indirectly through the use of intermediaries is no longer viable. They probably have already perceived that the prospect of fighting each other directly through nuclear confrontation is suicidal. Given these restructured perspectives the war system could become obsolete for the major powers.

Major power perception of war as obsolete could lead to the logical conclusion that the reciprocal limitation of arms under inspection safeguards is in the best interest both of the major powers and of the community. The military priority for resources can then freely yield to the dual priority of international and domestic development. Once competitive energies can be rerouted into non-violent channels,[5] the

[4] See International Law Commission, "Report to the General Assembly," *II Yearbook of the I. L. C. 1950* p. 317 (1957):

> Principle VII
>
> Complicity in the commission of a crime against peace, a war crime, or a crime against humanity as set forth in Principle VI is a crime under international law.

[5] On non-military competition see Millis, *The Abolition of War* 166 (1963):

> ... military power, as it has been developed by the elaborated organization of the modern state, no longer has any practical uses except in the search for power for its own sake ... the great national power centers may come to lay it aside in favor of the pursuit of other forms of power that may really be of some utility to their peoples.

But on global cooperation see *id.*, p. 200:

> The really basic interests ... call ... for global cooperation – in scientific technology, in economics, and in political order – if any is to enjoy the potential benefits of which the future gives promise to all.

See further Rabinowitch, "The Atomic Age Doctrine: Common Efforts for Common Aims," cite XVI *Bulletin of the Atomic Scientists* 259 (1960):

> ... a foreign policy with assistance to the needy parts of the world as the cornerstone, implies a fundamental change in the traditional foreign policy creed.... This creed has always been ... that the purpose of foreign policy of any nation is the furthering of its national interests ....
>
> The only proper aim of foreign policy in the atomic age is the furthering of the interests of mankind.

permanent members of the Security Council may be enabled to overcome the impediment to the unanimity required for the discharge of their primary responsibility for the maintenance of peace and security in the international community. The Security Council at last may effectuate its mandate.

And so we come around to the original vision of the nations which wrote the United Nations Charter and of the many other nations which have since put their signatures to it: a vision not of a monolithic government with a single control center, but of a system of order organized around a relatively few great centers of power which serve as the central agents of the community whose well-being is their trust.[6]

If the Security Council should find it possible to discharge its primary responsibility for the maintenance of international peace and security pursuant to Article 24 of the Charter, by effectively determining the existence of any threat to the peace, breach of the peace, or act of aggression pursuant to Article 39, the work of the Court may become superfluous or even incompatible with the role of the Council. The Court would then be prepared to yield to the primary responsibility of the Council. It is conceivable, however, that the Council would wish to make use of the distinctive qualification of the Court as an impartial determiner. In this case the Council could retain the services of the Court by adopting it as a subsidiary organ pursuant to Article 29, which says that:

> The Security Council may establish such subsidiary organs as it deems necessary for the performance of its functions.

Community Participation

Since man first learned warfare there has been need of law for the control of violence. When the community fails to provide for the legal protection of the general interest, one of its more influential members understandably may feel itself moved to supply the lack. Unilateral assumption of the peacekeeping responsibility, however, creates the risk that the self-appointee may confuse the general interest of the community with its particular interest. The lesson that has been paid for by painful experience is that the responsibility for the control of

[6] Cf. Millis, p. 201–02:

> How else can a working international power system be organized except through this concentration of power in a relatively few great centers, each unafraid of and militarily unthreatening to the others? The only obvious alternative is a global concentration under a single "world government" ... something impossible today and, even if it became possible, probably far less workable, desirable, or just than the situation envisaged by the authors of the United Nations.

violence has to be shared as broadly as possible among the entire membership of the community of nations. The ultimate duty is non-delegable. All nations must participate, as the Chief Justice of the United States saw clearly:

> Law building internationally is a program in which all nations can participate equally. All are therefore equally responsible for achievement of world peace through a world ruled by law. No nation can stand alone in today's interdependent world. We of the Americas are dependent upon you from Asia, Africa and Europe to help build peace and you are dependent upon us. Either we work together in building a world peace structure or that structure cannot be created.[7]

Conclusion

If the nations of the world can be persuaded to abandon the uncertain wait for major power accord, to repudiate the anachronism of judicial immunity for state-sponsored violence, and to graduate from nearly total reliance upon the military-economic-diplomatic instrument of influence to a legal instrument for the moral judgment of nations, they may yet discover a realistic way to extend the legal process to the resolution of the central problem confronting mankind in this era.

If this move is made, the majority of the world will no longer be reduced to the status of impotent spectators of the lawlessness which subverts the security of their society. No longer need the victim face the enormity of international violence with the options of watching in helpless resentment or of lashing out in violent self-help. At last he will get his case into court. And the peoples of the world will be there, as international due process comes alive on television screens around the globe.

An International Peace Court will offer a new venture in law to an old world with a dream:

> For out of Zion shall go forth the law,
> and the word of the Lord from Jerusalem.
> He shall judge between the nations,
> and shall decide for many peoples;
> and they shall beat their swords into plowshares,
> and their spears into pruning hooks;
> nation shall not lift up sword against nation,
> neither shall they learn war any more.[8]

[7] Warren, "Inaugural Adress," in World Peace Through Law Center, *World Peace Through Law, The Geneva World Conference* 41 (1969).

[8] Isaiah 2:3–4 (Revised Standard Version 1952).

EPILOGUE

The present proposal attempts a new arrangement upon an old theme. One of the great durables in the lore of the law, the theme is beautifully expressed at the inscription to be seen on the clock-tower of the Peace Palace at the Hague, seat of the World Court and home of the Academy of International Law, in these ancient syllables:

PACIS TUTELA APUD JUDICEM

APPENDIX

MODEL STATUTE FOR AN INTERNATIONAL PEACE COURT

Chapter I. General Principles

Article 1. Purpose of the Court

There is established an International Peace Court to adjudicate the legality under international law of acts of transnational violence perpetrated by the governments of national states.

Article 2. Law to be Applied by the Court

The Court shall apply international law, including the norms relating to transnational violence prescribed in the Charter Of The United Nations.

Article 3. Permanent Nature of the Court

The Court shall be a permanent body.

Chapter II. Organization of the Court

Article 4. Parties to the Statute of the International Peace Court

The states which are signatories of this Statute, or which shall later accede to it, are constituted the permanent supporting organization of the Court. They shall be designated the Parties to the Statute of the International Peace Court. Their function will be to administer the maintenance of the Court, except insofar as this function is entrusted to the Court by this Statute. In the discharge of their respective administrative functions the Parties to the Statute and the Court will operate by majority vote. They may delegate such executive responsibility and discretion as they choose to an Executive Secretary. The function of the Parties to the Statute is to provide for the maintenance of the Court. Its responsibilities will include the financial management of the Court, the administration of its physical amenities and the election of the judges.

The Executive Secretary will maintain his office at the permanent seat of the Court.

Article 5. Qualifications of Judges

The Court shall be composed of a body of independent judges, elected regardless of their nationality from among persons of high moral character, who possess the qualifications required in their respective countries for appointment to the highest judicial office, or are jurists of recognized competence in international law.

Article 6. Number of Judges

The Court shall consist of nine judges.

Article 7. Nationality of Judges

1. Judges may be elected from candidates of any nationality or without nationality.

2. No two judges may be nationals of the same State. A person who, for the purpose of membership in the Court, could be regarded as a national of more than one State shall be deemed to be a national of the State in which he ordinarily exercises civil and political rights.

Article 8. Representative Character of the Court

The electors shall bear in mind that the judges, as a body, should, as far as possible, represent the main forms of civilization and the principal legal systems of the world.

Article 9. Nomination of Candidates

1. Judges shall be elected from a list of candidates nominated by the Parties to the Statute.

2. Each of the Parties to the Statute may submit the names of not more than two candidates.

3. Before making these nominations, it is recommended that each Party consult its highest court of justice, its law school faculties, and its national associations and national sections of international associations devoted to the study and advancement of law.

Article 10. Invitation to Nominate

1. The date, time and place of each election shall be fixed by the Executive Secretary of the Parties to the Statute.

2. At least three months before this date, he shall address a written request to the Parties to the Statute, inviting them to undertake, within a time specified, the nomination of qualified persons in a position to accept the duties of a judge.

Article 11. List of Candidates

The Executive Secretary shall prepare a list, in alphabetical order, of all candidates. He shall submit the list to the Parties to the Statute.

Article 12. Election of Judges

1. The judges shall be elected at meetings of representatives of the Parties to the Statute. Candidates receiving the greatest number of votes will be elected. The Executive Secretary shall, after due notice to each of such states, convene these meetings.

2. In the event of more than one national of the same State obtaining a sufficient number of votes for election, the one who obtains the greatest number of votes shall be considered as elected and if the votes are equally divided the elder or eldest candidate shall be considered as elected.

Article 13. Terms of Office

1. The judges shall be elected for nine years and may be re-elected; provided, however, that of the judges elected at the first election, the terms of three judges shall expire at the end of three years and the terms of three more judges shall expire at the end of six years.

2. The judges whose terms are to expire at the end of the initial periods of three and six years shall be chosen by lot drawn by the Executive Secretary immediately after the first election has been completed.

3. Each judge whose term of office has expired shall continue to discharge his duties until his place has been filled. Though replaced, he shall finish any case which he may have begun.

4. In the case of the resignation of a judge, the resignation shall be addressed to the President of the Court, who shall transmit the resignation to the Executive Secretary.

Article 14. Solemn Declaration

Each judge shall, before taking up his duties, make a solemn declaration in open court that he will perform his functions impartially and conscientiously, and that he will preserve the secrecy of the Court's deliberations.

Article 15. Privileges and Immunities

1. The judges shall enjoy legal immunity for all acts performed by them in their official capacity.

2. Each judge, when engaged on the business of the Court, shall enjoy the diplomatic privileges and immunities accorded ambassadors.

Article 16. Occupations of Judges

1. No judge may act in any case other than as judge.

2. No judge may exercise any political or administrative function or engage in any other occupation of a professional nature.

3. No judge shall engage in any occupation which interferes with his judicial function during sessions of the Court. Nor shall he engage in any occupation which is incompatible with his functions as a judge.

4. Any doubt on these points shall be settled by the decision of the Court.

Article 17. Disability of Judges

1. No judge may participate in proceedings relating to any case in which he has previously taken part in any capacity whatsoever.

2. A judge of the nationality of one of the parties to a case shall not participate in the case.

3. Any doubt on these points shall be settled by the decision of the Court.

Article 18. Disqualifications of Judges

1. If, for some special reason, a judge considers that he should not participate in a particular proceeding, he shall so inform the President.

2. Any party to a proceeding may submit that a judge should not participate in the proceeding. Such submission shall be addressed to the President.

3. If the President, upon receipt of such submission or of his own motion, considers that a judge should not participate in a particular proceeding, the President shall so advise the judge.

4. If the President and the judge disagree on the issue, the Court shall decide.

Article 19. Dismissal of Judges

1. No judge shall be dismissed unless, in the unanimous opinion of

the other judges, he has ceased to fulfil the conditions required for his continuance in the office.

2. Formal notification of such unanimous opinion shall be made to the Executive Secretary by the Registrar of the Court.

3. Thereupon the dismissed judge shall immediately cease to perform all functions as a member of the Court.

Article 20. Vacancies

1. Vacancies shall be filled by the same method as that prescribed for the first election. The Executive Secretary shall, within one month of the occurrence of a vacancy, issue the invitations provided for in Article 10.

2. A judge elected to replace a judge whose term of office has not expired shall hold office for the remainder of his predecessor's term.

Article 21. Officers

1. The Court shall elect its President and Vice-President for three years; each may be re-elected.

2. The Court may appoint one or two court advocates, whose function shall be to present publicly and with complete impartiality and independence reasoned arguments on the cases submitted to the Court.

3. The Court shall appoint its Registrar and shall provide for the appointment of such other officers and personnel as may be necessary.

4. The Court shall define the duties of the Registrar and other officers and personnel, and supervise their execution.

Article 22. Seat of the Court

1. The permanent seat of the Court shall be established at Geneva, Switzerland. The Court may, however, sit and exercise its functions elsewhere whenever the Court considers it desirable.

2. The judges, court advocates, if any, Registrar and other officers shall reside at the seat of the Court.

Article 23. Sessions

1. The Court shall remain permanently in session.

2. Judges are entitled to individual periodic leave, the dates and duration of which shall be fixed by the Court, having in mind the distance between the permanent seat of the Court and the home of the individual judge. The dates of leave should be arranged so as to

maintain at least a quorum of judges at the seat of the Court at all times.

3. Judges shall be bound, unless they are on leave or prevented from attending by illness or other serious reasons acceptable to the President, to hold themselves permanently at the disposal of the Court.

Article 24. Attendance and Quorum

1. A full court shall sit, except when less than the full membership is available.

2. In the absence of the President, the Vice-President shall act as President.

3. A quorum of five judges shall suffice to constitute the Court.

4. The Court shall sit validly only with an uneven number of judges.

Article 25. Emoluments

1. Each judge shall receive an annual salary.

2. The President shall receive a special annual allowance.

3. The Vice-President shall receive a special allowance for every day on which he acts as a President.

4. These salaries and allowances shall be fixed by the Parties to the Statute.

5. The Court Advocates, if any, Registrar, other officers and personnel of the Court shall receive annual salaries as fixed by the Parties to the Statute.

6. The Parties to the Statute shall have discretion to fix the terms and conditions of retirement pensions, official expenses and benefits of all Court personnel.

Article 26. Finances

1. The expenses of the Court shall be borne by the Parties to the Statute.

2. The Parties to the Statute shall create and maintain a fund to be collected and administered in accordance with regulations adopted by them. From this fund shall be paid all expenses.

3. A State which is not one of the Parties to the Statute, and which, as complainant, engages the services of the Court, may be asked by the Parties to make a proportionate voluntary monetary contribution within its means.

Article 27. Rules of the Court

1. The Court shall adopt rules for directing its functions. In particu-

lar, it shall prescribe rules of procedure and such general principles governing proof and evidence as the Court may deem necessary.

2. Rules and amendments shall be published before becoming effective, and shall not be altered so as to affect pending proceedings.

Chapter III. Jurisdiction of Parties and Subject Matter

Article 28. Parties Litigant and Subject Matter

1. Only the governments of nation-states may appear as parties litigant in cases before the Court.

2. A state which files a complaint accusing another state of transnational violence shall be the complainant, and the accused state shall be the defendant.

3. In exceptional circumstances, such as the use of duress against an aggrieved state, the Court may authorize another state or group of states to appear as surrogate complainant on behalf of the aggrieved state.

4. The subject matter of the Court's jurisdiction shall be limited to acts of violence which are sponsored by the government of a nation-state, and which affect persons or property outside its territory, in any case submitted by a party complainant.

5. The non-appearance of a party defendant shall not affect the Court's jurisdiction over the subject matter or its competence to decide on the merits. A party defendant shall be invited but not compelled to appear.

6. The Registrar shall send to the chief executive officer or to the legislature of a non-appearing party defendant certified copies of the complaint, minutes of all hearings as they occur and the judgment.

Article 29. Jurisdictional Disputes

In the event of a dispute as to whether the Court has jurisdiction, the matter shall be settled by the decision of the Court.

Chapter IV. Procedure

Article 30. Language

1. The official languages of the Court shall be French and English. The language of the case shall be by agreement of the parties to the case.

2. In the absence of an agreement as to which language shall be

employed, each party may, in the pleadings, use the language which it prefers, and the decision of the Court shall be given in both languages, that text being authoritative as so determined by the Court.

3. The Court may, at the request of any party litigant, authorize a language other than French or English to be used by that party.

Article 31. Representation

1. The parties litigant shall be represented by agents.

2. They may have the assistance of counsel.

3. Agents and counsel shall enjoy the privileges and immunities necessary to the independent exercise of their office.

Article 32. Commencement of Action

1. A case shall be brought before the Court by filing a written complaint with the Registrar.

2. The complaint shall contain a concise statement of the facts which constitute each alleged offense and a specific reference to the law under which the defendant is charged.

Article 33. Proceedings

1. The proceedings shall consist of two parts, written and oral.

2. The written part of the proceedings shall consist of the complaint by the complainant, the answer by the defendant, and, if necessary, a further reply by the complainant.

3. These pleadings shall be filed with the Registrar, in the order and within the time fixed by the Court.

4. A certified copy of every pleading filed by one party shall be remitted to the other party.

5. Upon application of the defendant, the Court may require complainant to submit a bill of particulars in detailed specification of the allegations of the complaint.

6. The oral part of the proceedings shall consist of the hearing by the Court of witnesses, experts, agents and counsel.

7. The Court may authorize amendment or withdrawal of the complaint.

8. Decisions of the Court shall be in writing and shall state the reasons on which they are based.

Article 34. Hearings

1. The hearing shall be under the control of the President, or, if he is unable to preside, the Vice-President.

2. If neither is able to preside, the senior judge shall preside.

3. The hearing shall be public unless there are exceptional circumstances in which the Court finds that public sittings might prejudice the interests of justice.

4. Minutes shall be made of each hearing and signed by the Registrar and the President.

5. These minutes alone shall be authentic.

Article 35. Evidence at Hearing and in Preliminary Inquiry

1. The Court shall make orders for the conduct of the case, shall decide the form and time in which each party must present its arguments, and make all arrangements connected with the taking of evidence.

2. The Court shall, before public hearing begins, call upon agents or counsel to produce any document and supply any explanations bearing on the reasonableness of the complaint. A complaint which is not *prima facie* reasonable shall be dismissed. This preliminary inquiry may be conducted in secret in order to protect any innocent party litigant or government.

3. Formal note shall be taken of any refusal of evidence.

4. The court may entrust any person or organization with the task of making an inquiry or of giving an expert opinion.

5. When, subject to the Court's control, the agents and counsel have completed their presentation of evidence, the President shall declare the hearing closed.

Article 36. Deliberation

1. The Court shall withdraw to consider the judgment.

2. The deliberations of the Court shall take place in private and remain secret.

3. All questions shall be decided by majority vote of the judges present.

4. In the event of a tie vote, made possible by the absence from the deliberation of a judge who participated in the hearing, the presiding judge shall have a casting vote.

Article 37. Judgment

1. The Court shall give judgment either of acquittal or of censure.

2. The judgment shall state the reasons on which it is based.

3. It shall name the judges who have taken part in the deliberation.

4. If the judgment does not represent in whole or in part, as to the decision or as to the reasons, the opinion of any of the deliberating judges, any such judge shall be entitled to deliver a separate opinion.

5. The judgment shall be signed by the President and certified by the Registrar. It shall be read in open Court, due notice having been given to the parties to the case, their agents and counsel.

6. The judgment shall be designated by the Court as final or provisional.

7. A provisional judgment shall be automatically reviewed and either made final or vacated after expiration of a time period as the Court shall have prescribed and upon determination of the defendant's compliance with such terms of good conduct as the Court shall have laid down.

8. The Court shall interpret the meaning of any judgment upon request of a party litigant.

Article 38. Default Judgment

1. Whenever a defendant does not appear before the Court, or fails to defend its case, the complainant may call upon the Court to decide on its complaint.

2. The Court must, before doing so, satisfy itself that it has jurisdiction, and that the complaint is well founded in fact and in law through hearings on the merits attended by counsel appointed by the Court to represent the defendant.

Article 39. Appeal

Any judgment of censure may be appealed to such reviewing tribunal and in such manner as the Parties to the Statute may provide for.

Article 40. Revision and Vacation of Judgment

1. The Court may reconsider a judgment at any time upon submission of new evidence which was unknown to the Court when the judgment was given.

2. Denial of such reconsideration shall be appealable in keeping with Article 39.

3. The Court may, in its discretion, vacate a final judgment after the expiration of ten years from its entry, upon application of the adjudged government and proof that its interim international conduct has, in the consideration of the Court, been of such high standard as to merit vacation of the judgment.

4. Denial of such application shall not be appealable.

5. Before vacating a judgment, the Court may in its discretion require the applicant to comply with special conditions, such as the making of reparations for its past transnational injuries, or the making of other contributions to the international commonweal.

Article 41. Special Legal Issues

1. If a case involves a complex issue of a civil legal nature which is part of the background of the alleged act of transnational violence and integral to the determination of the case, the Court may refer the parties litigant to another tribunal for special determination of this issue.

2. Upon the failure of the parties litigant to accept the reference to a second tribunal pursuant to paragraph 1 and after consideration both of its own resources and of the interests of justice in the light of both the special issue and the principal issue raised by the complaint, the Court will have the option either of continuing with the principal case or of disqualifying itself and dismissing the complaint.

3. Should a state which is not a party consider that it has an interest of a legal nature which may be affected by the decision of the case, it may submit a request to the Court to be permitted to intervene.

4. It shall be for the Court to decide upon this request.

5. Any judgment of the Court shall be limited to a determination of the existence and legality of an act of state-sponsored transnational violence.

6. No other issue shall receive final legal determination in the Court.

7. Subsequent resolution at any time, in any tribunal, of any legal issue bearing upon the merits of a case which has gone to judgment in the Court, shall be grounds for reopening the principal case, subject to the Court's discretion, for possible revision, including voidance, pursuant to the terms of Article 40 (1 and 2).

Article 42. Rights of the Defendant

1. The defendant shall be presumed innocent until proven guilty.

2. The defendant shall have a fair trial and, in particular:

(a) The right to be present through its agent at all stages of the proceedings;

(b) The right to conduct its own defense or to be defended by counsel of its own choice, and to have its counsel present at all stages of the proceedings; and if it does not have counsel of choice, the right to have counsel appointed and, if necessary, remunerated by the Court, such appointment of counsel to be mandatory before a judgment be taken;

(c) The right to have the proceedings of the Court, including documentary evidence, translated into its own language;

(d) The right to interrogate any witness and to inspect any document or other evidence introduced during the trial;

(e) The right to adduce oral and other evidence in its defense;

(f) The right to the assistance of the Court in obtaining access to material in the complainant's control which the Court is satisfied may be relevant to the issues before the Court.

3. The defendant shall have the right to be heard through its agent or counsel. It shall be liable to questioning by the Court and by counsel. It shall not be compelled to take an oath.

4. If the Court considers it impossible to ensure a fair trial, the Court may, by a decision supported by reasons, suspend the proceedings and if they are not resumed within a time limit determined by the Court, dismiss the case.

Chapter V. Amendment and Participation

Article 43. Amendment

1. The present Statute may be amended by majority vote of the Parties to the Statute.

2. The Court may propose amendments through written communication to the Executive Secretary.

Article 44. Participation

1. The present Statute shall be open to participation by all nation-states.

2. It shall enter into force upon deposit with the depository government of the requisite number of ratifications.

3. The depository government shall be —————.

4. The requisite number of ratifications shall be ————.

AUTHOR INDEX

SUBJECT INDEX

GPSR Compliance

The European Union's (EU) General Product Safety Regulation (GPSR) is a set of rules that requires consumer products to be safe and our obligations to ensure this.

If you have any concerns about our products, you can contact us on ProductSafety@springernature.com

In case Publisher is established outside the EU, the EU authorized representative is:

Springer Nature Customer Service Center GmbH
Europaplatz 3
69115 Heidelberg, Germany

Batch number: 10830943

Printed by Printforce, the Netherlands